Self-Publishing 101

Debbie Elicksen

Self-Counsel Press
(a division of)
International Self-Counsel Press Ltd.
USA   Canada

Self-Counsel Press acknowledges the financial support of the Government of Canada through the Book Publishing Industry Development Program (BPIDP) for our publishing activities.

Printed in Canada.

First edition: 2005

Library and Archives Canada Cataloguing in Publication

Elicksen, Debbie
   Self-publishing 101 / Debbie Elicksen. — 1st ed.

(Self-counsel reference series)
ISBN 1-55180-639-8

   1. Self-publishing. I. Title. II. Series.

Z285.5.E44 2005   070.5'93   C2005-905641-X

Self-Counsel Press
(a division of)
International Self-Counsel Press Ltd.

1704 North State Street	1481 Charlotte Road
Bellingham, WA 98225	North Vancouver, BC V7J 1H1
USA	Canada

Contents

APPENDIXES

SAMPLES

TABLES

Notice to Readers

Acknowledgments

It's impossible to embark on an undertaking such as writing this book without the kind words of support from colleagues and friends: thank you, Donna Matheson, Audrey Bakewell, Don and Molly Henderson, Janice Delude, Donna Armstrong, Pamela and Daniel Clark, Dave Rowe, Colleen Connolly, Mette Juliussen, Peter Watts, Sharon Eberson, Nadien Cole, Art Breeze, and, especially, Stan Fischler.

A special thank-you to Richard Day, Barbara Kuhne, Audrey McClellan, Jill Lublin, Rob Lennard, Lyle Manery, Burton Colter, Peter Friebel, Tom Douglas, Bruce Dowbiggin, Ron and Adrianna Edwards, and Warren Redman. And to others too numerous to mention who provided input, thank you.

Foreword

Debbie Elicksen's *Self-Publishing 101* is a direct and forthright book about the basics of self-publishing, filled with highly useful information.

Debbie makes it clear that it is not enough just to "write a book." For starters, your written material must be edited, and she illustrates this truism with poignant humor. You also need a great cover that includes a title that is imaginative and informative.

Debbie guides you through the steps that follow the creation of your gem — the result of your toil and, in many cases, great struggle. You may breathe a sigh of relief that you are finally ready to unveil your masterpiece to a waiting audience. Well, you will soon discover you have only just begun. You are not at the end of this journey into publishing — you are at the beginning.

Perhaps you, like most authors, hope someone will take your precious words and carry them through the publishing process. That may happen, but it is rarely ever quite so easy.

Self-Publishing 101 reviews the pros and cons of the basic types of publishing: royalty or traditional publishing, vanity presses, print-on-demand publishing, and self-publishing.

In the past, self-publishing was equated with defeat. People had the idea that if a royalty publisher did not put its stamp of approval on your work, it must not be good enough. However, if you look at the list of famous and incredibly successful authors who are self-published, you must admit that the common perception is flawed.

Self-Publishing 101 does not try to convince you that *you* should self-publish. It simply assumes it is one of the basic approaches you should know about. The message the reader should glean from this book is that the publishing process is the same whether you manage to get someone else to do some of the essential steps or you do it all yourself.

The difference between self-publishing and all the other styles is a matter of control. Depending on which way your book is published, you must give up some portion of control. With self-publishing you control the words, the layout, the color of the cover, and all that really matters to you.

This is a most timely book because more and more authors are using self-publishing as the preferred method for getting their books into print. Debbie provides the fundamentals necessary to get the would-be author/self-publisher off to a great start.

How I wish such a resource had been available to me when I self-published my first book over ten years ago.

— *Lyle Manery*

Author and self-publisher of more than ten books, including the bestseller *No Salesman Will Call?*, as well as numerous articles and short stories.

Introduction

In 2001, when I had been covering the National Hockey League (NHL) as a freelance writer for about ten years, I knew the time had come to elevate my credibility as a sports writer, to try and set myself on the same level as a beat reporter. To achieve this, I decided to write a book — a book that both NHL personnel (players, owners, coaches, scouts, etc.) and fans would want to buy. My primary goals were to —

- raise my profile as an NHL reporter;

- inspire NHLers with my book so that if any of them decided they wanted to tell their stories, they would choose me to help them write their book; and

- sell books.

What qualified me to write a book in the first place? I had been a published writer for many years, and my articles appeared in numerous local, national, and international publications. At the same time, I have had a long career in sports media and administration. That experience has included working in administration for amateur and professional hockey, baseball, and football, as well as volunteering with the Hockey Media Committee for the 1988 Olympic Winter Games. I also represent the Calgary Chamber of Commerce on the City of Calgary Sport Policy Steering Committee.

I played a key role in junior football in Canada for 18 years and was the first woman to lead a football conference in Canada as president of the Prairie Football Conference. As president and assistant general manager of the Calgary Colts and an executive of the Canadian Junior Football League, I became known as a strong administrator, lobbying for on-field and off-field improvements throughout the league. My football duties included overseeing game-day operations, overseeing business and football operations, managing public relations, assisting in equipment management, making team travel arrangements, negotiating coaching salaries, and even negotiating a team into the conference.

As public relations director for the Edmonton Trappers Triple A Baseball Club, I worked closely with the California Angels, the Trappers' parent club, and was responsible for overseeing game-day operations, media liaison, staff, statistics, player requests, and community events.

As a reporter, I touch on the human side of the players and people who work inside sports, the part of the game most people never get to see. My approach may be unique as a result of two factors: I'm a woman and I'm a former sports administrator. I regularly cover the Calgary Flames and the National Hockey League, the Calgary Stampeders and the Canadian Football League, the Calgary Roughnecks and the National Lacrosse League, as well as other sports. I have filed reports for *The Fischler Report* and ESPN *SportsTicker,* among others.

My lucky break came in the early 1980s when famed hockey writer Stan Fischler asked me to help him research his book *The Great Gretzky.* Stan has authored over 100 books, mostly about hockey. He has been a valuable mentor to me and taught me a great deal about book publishing. He gave me the chance to work in the NHL, thus opening the door to many other opportunities.

Before I developed *Inside the NHL Dream,* I mapped out a detailed business plan. I figured that creating a book was such an investment of time (and money) that it should be approached the same way I approached designing my website — as if I were starting a new business.

I determined who would read the book, how I would market it, and when I should publish it. Because I was so passionate about what I was writing, the one thing I knew for sure was I had to have total control over the entire project. I didn't want a traditional publisher. I didn't want to risk losing editorial or creative control.

I also knew it couldn't look like a self-published book. Curb appeal was everything. It had to be well edited and professionally designed. Looks are everything to a book's credibility — especially a first book.

I was determined to write this book, even after I was struck by a car in a downtown Calgary crosswalk. Even though my injuries sucked away my energy and concentration and I couldn't work as much as usual, I had to publish this book, no matter what. I borrowed and begged to come up with the funding, maxing out credit cards and favors. I wasn't going to use anything — not poor health, not lack of money — as an excuse to abandon this book.

It was an expensive venture. I spent thousands of dollars needlessly on the education process. I was burned several times because of my naïveté. (On the positive side, this steep and costly learning curve made my next two books much easier to produce.)

For example, I knew I needed a distributor to get my books into a bookstore, so when a woman called me from Traverse City, Michigan, to offer her services, I signed the agreement (after a lawyer perused the contract). The editor of *WritersWeekly* warned against becoming involved with a distributor who charged up-front costs, but by then it was too late.

The distributor's contract said her fee would be only 10 percent of the retail cost for each book she sold, but I had to purchase an advertisement in her catalogue (which was not distributed until nearly six months after initiating the contract). The distributor claimed she represented publishers at the BookExpo America book fair, which was taking place about two months later, so there was an urgency to come up with the US$800 (translating to CDN$1,300 at the time) for the ad. I sold my car — my beautiful baby, which I deeply loved. That's how badly I needed to publish this book.

After many months, this distributor had not sold any books for any of the publishers she carried. She phoned and e-mailed me from time to time, directing me to send a book, by courier, to legitimate US media sources, but there were no resulting book sales. Meanwhile, my Canadian distributor had books in 350 Chapters stores nationwide within three weeks.

While some of the mistakes I made were huge in terms of money, I did a lot of things right when I published that first book because I diligently researched the process and asked questions of those who had already self-published.

As a result, I put an effective marketing/promotion plan in place. I developed an e-flyer that I sent to every sports media outlet in North America. I sent as many as 200 e-mails a day to hockey teams, leagues, and organizations; media; corporations (that could use the book as a gift); and anyone else even distantly connected to hockey. Because I was in the media myself, I had one advantage: I had immediate access to other media and NHL personnel on whom I wanted to make an impression. I managed to land three major national television spots that were instrumental in putting this book on the map.

I probably used 200 books for promotional purposes. Each person I interviewed for the book received a copy with a handwritten thank-you card expressing my appreciation for his or her time. Several high-profile media people received a copy, as did many influential NHL-types, such as team presidents, scouts, and league executives.

In under two years, my efforts to get noticed were starting to pay off. I sold a lot of books, but not so many that I no longer had to work. (Myth Number One: writers make enough money that they're able to retire.) People did come forward to ask me to help them with their books, but not just people from the sporting world. Readers, business associates, networking groups, and associations constantly asked me questions about the process. In fact, I received so many queries about publishing that, urged on by the prompting of a friend, I started to hold workshops on book publishing. I've since launched an e-newsletter, *Inside Publishing*, that provides helpful tips and resources, particularly for those who are novices to the publishing industry.

I couldn't ignore what was happening. People seemed to need this information; they needed to be leveled with and not deceived with the line, "If you work with me, your book will be a bestseller." I told them the truth — what you put in is what you get out. Many time-stressed people paid me to help them through the process. It was my lap into which they dumped their manuscripts to have them turned into books. They appreciated the "do it professionally or don't do it at all" approach.

I decided to take this message to a larger arena. Enter Self-Counsel Press. I love the irony of placing a book about self-publishing with a traditional publisher. Because my message has touched on both publishing worlds, this was a perfect partnership in the making.

Self-Publishing 101 will help you understand the traditional publishing world and why it's so difficult to get published. You'll learn about other publishing options. And you'll learn the ins and outs of producing a professional-looking book, how to get it into the bookstores, and how to promote and sell it outside the bookstores.

My goal for this book is to elevate the professionalism of self-publishers by explaining the steps you should take to produce a good-looking, well-written book that people will want to pick up and pay for. Even if you end up with a traditional publishing contract, I hope this book will smooth your way through the publishing process by giving you a good idea of what to expect.

This book will also dispel many of the myths of book publishing. What you will learn is that regardless of how a book is published, writing a book is about sales and the reader, not the author or the publisher. It's a sobering fact, but if you know this going in and learn how to set yourself apart from the other books on the shelf, you'll be able to write your way to success.

1

So You Want to Be a Writer

> *Whether a boy will grow up to be a firefighter or a physician, an architect or a teacher, his success will probably depend on his ability to communicate through written language.*
>
> WILLIAM POLLACK, REAL BOYS

Being a writer is like being an actor. The Al Pacinos and Meryl Streeps paid their dues by working other jobs, showing up for auditions, and grabbing whatever experience they could to shape their resumes. They even worked for free.

One of the most successful modern writers, J.K. Rowling, author of the Harry Potter series, was an unemployed single mother living on public assistance when she wrote *Harry Potter and the Philosopher's Stone.* She penned the bulk of her novel at a café table during her daughter's naps. The manuscript was rejected by at least one agent before another company took it on, and then it was sent to several publishers before Bloomsbury accepted it and ended up with a huge phenomenon on its hands.

Unfortunately, despite the example of J.K. Rowling, there is no get-rich-quick scheme for becoming a writer. It's about the

If you want to be a writer, there's only one thing to do. Write.

process. Sometimes it's a matter of just getting started. For many, that's the biggest challenge of all.

If you want to be a writer, there's only one thing to do. Write. Write every day. Start a journal. Don't worry about style and flow at the beginning. Just get in the habit of writing.

Write what you know. Coming up with book ideas starts in your own backyard. Jill Lublin is the co-author of *Guerrilla Publicity* and *Networking Magic.* She is a renowned strategist and international speaker, CEO of the strategic consulting firm Promising Promotion, and the founder of GoodNews Media, a company specializing in positive news. She is currently the host of the nationally syndicated radio show *Do the Dream,* on which she interviews celebrities who have achieved their dreams. Jill also has a television pilot, *GoodNews TV.*

"I came up with the idea for my book because I was an expert in publicity and actually doing it for people for over 20 years," says Jill. "I wanted to put all my information into a book form to make it simple for other businesspeople, entrepreneurs, speakers, and authors to do their own publicity without spending a fortune."

Sometimes book ideas are clear in the author's mind. Other times, "writer's block" sets in. There are several books that can help you get started. For example, books like *What If? Writing Exercises for Fiction Writers* by Anne Bernays and Pamela Painter and *A Writer's Workbook: Daily Exercises for the Writing Life* by Caroline Sharp contain simple exercises to help you tap into your own experiences and use your creativity to write in descriptive detail. (See Appendix 1 for more detail on these books and other publishing and writing resources.)

Even if you have an idea for a book, you may not know how to get started. To get unstuck, read. Read both fiction and nonfiction, regardless of which direction you intend to go in your own writing. Reading allows you to become more creative with your thoughts and expression. It gives you ideas.

Take note of other writers' styles when you read. Look at their opening lines. Do they grab your attention with the first sentence or do you have to read to page 100 before you can get into the story? How do they close a chapter? How do they shape their introduction?

Keep notebooks handy, especially beside your bed or in the car. When an idea comes to you, you must write it down immediately — even if it's 3 a.m. If you don't, it's gone. You'll never get it back. Some of my best ideas have come in the middle of the night or in the shower. It can be an opening sentence, a title, or an idea for a book. It's tough when it happens in the shower. I'll repeat it over and over until I get out, and then I'll write it down, even if I'm dripping wet.

A pocket tape recorder works well in lieu of a notepad. Such a recorder costs between $40 and $60 and the microcassette tapes are quite inexpensive. Keep it with you everywhere to record ideas as they occur to you.

When you do have an idea for a book, don't wait until you have it all mapped out before you start writing. Keep in mind that, just as movies aren't filmed in sequence, books aren't generally researched or written in chapter order. Just make sure you get everything down "on paper" first. As you're researching a particular part of the book, or thinking about a particular scene in a novel, you might have a brain wave about how to present it. Start writing. You can't be sure of remembering the bright idea when you get to that part of the book.

If writing stuff down seems overwhelming, or if your hectic schedule makes it difficult to sit down at your computer, use a pocket tape recorder and dictate the chapters into it. Stockpile the tapes until you're ready to transcribe. You may have to do more than the usual amount of editing, but what matters is getting started.

Don't forget to back up everything you write on your computer. It's nearly impossible to rewrite from memory. Back up onto two separate disks and print off a hard copy. One of the disks should be stored off-site. After all, what good is a backup if the house burns down or a hurricane hits? You might even take the step of e-mailing the manuscript to yourself every time you update it. That way, if the worst happens, you can access your e-mail off-site.

Also, be sure to save your work as you go. I usually save after every paragraph or couple of sentences. It's not that tedious when you think about what might happen should the power suddenly go off. Call it preventive medicine. That extra second it takes to mouse your pointer to the Save icon or hit Ctrl+S will save you endless grief.

Besides backing up your work, you must protect your intellectual property at all times by having the most up-to-date antivirus software protection, firewall protection, and spyware protection. Even with the most up-to-date protection, gremlins can still get in, so it's important to scan your computer regularly for worms, viruses, and other nasties.

Have Something to Say That Readers Want to Hear

Why are you writing a book? What do you want it to accomplish? How do you want to be remembered?

This is something you need to address before you begin. Remember, you're looking at hundreds of hours and perhaps one or two years of time invested, with no guarantees that anyone will read the resulting manuscript.

Never write a book for the sake of writing a book. Who cares? Who is going to read it? Everyone wants to write a book. What makes yours special? What do you have to offer the world? What experiences can you share that might help or encourage others? What is your expertise? Why would someone be interested in your story?

Your book must have something to offer readers because, in reality, it's about them, not you. What do they want to read? What do they need? Your book could be entertaining, funny, a good story. It could offer tips on business, inspiration, or expert commentary on a topical subject. But you won't sell a single copy if it doesn't appeal to readers. It doesn't matter what the book is about, it has to be written for the reader. Perhaps the best measure is to ask yourself, if someone else wrote the same book, would I read it?

Write What You Know — Or Do Your Research

According to Richard North Patterson, author of *No Safe Place:*

> Writing is akin to method acting. Before a writer can render a fully convincing world, he must inhabit that world and every major character that lives there.

Whether your book is science fiction, nonfiction, or a children's book, make it believable. Do your homework. Since Starbucks was established in 1971, you wouldn't use it as a backdrop for a story about the 1950s rock 'n' roller Buddy Holly who died in 1959. If you are writing about something that happened during the US Civil War, research what it was like to live in those times. What did people wear? What did they eat? How did they make a living?

If you are writing nonfiction, use real-life examples, statistics, and expert testimony to bring your argument to life.

Write what you know. Write what you're passionate about. When you do, it comes across to the reader.

Make your book personal in the sense that it's your work, even if it's filled with expert interviews. Quotations can strengthen your argument, but if you put a quote from a famous person in every paragraph, the reader might get the impression you're just filling up space. Make sure material you use from other people — whether it's drawn from conversation, formal interviews, books, or articles — is relevant to your subject and to the point you're making.

Depending on the circumstances under which your book is being published, if you feel you must quote more than one or two lines from another author's writing, you will have to request permission to use the material from that author's publisher. (See Sample 1 for an example of a letter requesting permission to reprint.) You may or may not get an answer. If you don't receive a response, or if permission is denied, go to Plan B: get creative and use your own words.

There is a difference between borrowing ideas and plagiarism. Plagiarism is passing off someone else's creation as your own. Obviously, writers quote other writers' works all the time. The difference is that they also credit those writers and indicate where the material came from. Plagiarism is serious business. Make sure, if you use another writer's quote, that you cite the source (the author and where it came from). Theft of someone else's written work is a one-way ticket to the reject pile, if not to the courtroom.

Many people can come up with the same idea at the same time, but not all of them will act on it. Ideas cannot be copyrighted until they are put into a physical form. Then it's the physical form that's copyrightable (the text, song, movie, etc.), not the idea. (That's why there are so many books and movies with the same basic theme, but all worked out in different ways.)

SAMPLE 1
SAMPLE PERMISSION REQUEST LETTER

July 30, 20--

Permissions Manager
All-Star Publishing
111 First Place Road
New York, NY 11110

Dear Permissions Manager:

I'd like to request permission to (reprint, republish, copy, distribute, or use) the following material:

- Title, Author, Copyright Date, ISBN if applicable

- Pages as they appear in the publication

- Text, distinguishing characteristics if image, URL for web page content, etc.

The material will appear in my upcoming book, *Self-Publishing for Everyone*, which will be published in October 20-- by My Publishing Company. I plan to limit the use of your material to (the book's text, marketing/promotional materials, etc.) and will not use it any other way.

I'm hoping you will grant me permission to use this material for my book or put me in touch with the person who would authorize this request. I would appreciate receiving your response to this permission request by August 31, 20--

Sincerely,

I.M.A. Writer

Find a Niche

You don't want your book to be like everyone else's. Perhaps you have an idea of the type of book you want to write, you know why you want to write it, but you haven't quite mastered the theme. Most of the time, we find our book topics from our own experiences and in the people we know.

Warren Redman is a professional speaker, coach, trainer, and president of the Centre for Inner Balancing. He has written 15 books, 3 of them self-published, including *The 9 Steps to Emotional Fitness* and *Achieving Personal Success:*

> All my books have arisen from my experience and the development of ideas, concepts, and practices that worked for me. The book writing was a natural progression and continuation of my learning and desire to share that learning with a wider audience.

Tom Douglas is an award-winning journalist and author who once worked as communications advisor for Veterans Affairs Canada. He has produced four books, one self-published and three with Altitude Publishing. His book *Canadian Spies* has sold over 19,000 copies. He describes how he came up with his topics:

> I wrote a feature about my mother trying to find Christmas presents that my inebriated father had mistakenly thrown out in the garbage. The local Ontario Provincial Police constable took her to the garbage dump, where she rooted around with her bare hands. She didn't find them, but the story had a definitely happy ending. I submitted it to the *Toronto Star* and they ran it as a Christmas article one year. The next year I submitted a second Christmas story about a German refugee giving me his old lead toy soldiers as an exchange gift in grade three. My wife, Gail, encouraged me to set down other childhood memories in print, hence the book *Some Sunny Day.* When I couldn't get a publisher to take on the manuscript, I went to Booklocker.com in the United States, and they published it at my expense. I sold about 500 copies to friends, relatives, and attendees at several book readings.

Most often, we find book topics from our own experience.

The *Toronto Star* was also instrumental in my publishing *Canadian Spies* with Altitude. I had met some French-Canadian veterans in 1984 when I was communications assistant to the minister of Veterans Affairs. We traveled to Brittany together for a ceremony where the French government honored these heroes for risking their lives to save downed Allied airmen. When a radio personality criticized French-Canadians as being cowardly, in an article picked up by the *Star*, I wrote a letter to the editor about the exploits of the men I had met. I pitched the story to Altitude Publishing, and they bought it.

D-Day was a natural follow-up. It was a tribute to my dad and the others who served in World War II. Also, to reveal my crass side, it was written to capitalize on [the] 60th anniversary of D-Day.

Great Canadian War Heroes resulted from a request by Altitude to keep my successful run of military books going.

While Tom Douglas wrote from his personal experiences and passions, Lyle Manery used his business experience to pen a book. Both kept the reader in mind. Lyle Manery is a chartered life underwriter, chartered financial consultant, speaker, coach, life member of the Million Dollar Round Table, and two-time Top of the Table member. He has authored 11 books, including *Laughing at Life* and *The Ultimate Tax Shelter*. His self-published book, *No Salesman Will Call?*, sold over 5,000 copies:

In 1992–93, there was a company that advertised on TV in an attempt to sell direct to the public. They finished each advertisement with, "No commissioned salesperson will call." That irritated me. The prospective buyer would have to talk with *someone*, and that person would get paid to make sales. That company was denigrating commissioned salespeople, even though they are better qualified. Hence, the title.

Beyond that, there were a large number of books and articles being written which attacked the life insurance product, the companies that designed the product, and the agents who sold it. Invariably, one point of attack made by each and every author was about commissions. These authors had no credentials to write about the life insurance industry or its products. Certainly, they did not have a right to generalize about the intentions of all agents.

Why do people accept the words from a CA [Chartered Accountant], just because he has an unrelated certificate? Why would anyone agree with just any pronouncement from a college professor of English or of business administration? These people do not necessarily know about everything merely because they know more than most people about something. Why does a celebrity, a doctor, a lawyer, an actor, or an author take on an air of importance in the public's mind? What right do these people have to advise people on topics outside their areas of expertise?

In *No Salesman Will Call?*, I critiqued over 55 authors and writers whose books and articles were sheer nonsense. No one else was prepared to answer them — so I did it!

Ron and Adrianna Edwards are the principals of Focus Strategic Communications Incorporated, a full-service communications firm that offers book-packaging production and marketing services to the book publishing industry. They also function as literary agents. Between the two of them, they have nearly 50 years' experience in publishing and marketing communications.

How do they come up with ideas for book projects?

There is no simple answer to this, but the short answer is that we look for gaps. Start by doing your homework. Study the catalogs of the publishers you are interested in working for and see what is missing. Then develop an idea to fill the gaps. The more radical or nontraditional your idea, the harder the sell will be. Publishers are a very conservative lot and are not, by and large, big risk takers. They want new and unique ideas but in a traditional, conservative vein.

To come up with your own niche, ask yourself the following questions:

- What do you do that is different from everyone else?
- What advice do you get asked for all the time?
- What are you most known for?
- What do you know for sure?
- If your book is about business, why do customers buy your service?
- What are your business's strengths and weaknesses?
- What are some historic trends in an industry, profession, city, region, or other niche?
- How has a topic changed over the years? For example, how is medicine and the way it's delivered to patients different today than it was in the 1950s?
- What are some of the challenges you faced while growing your business, raising your kids, learning to overcome a disability?
- How do your management skills impact your staff, your household environment, or your ability to cope with challenges?
- What is your role in the industry you work in?
- Why do people find you fascinating?
- What do you say to those just starting out in a new venture, from marriage to business to a hobby?
- What isn't being said about the industry you work in?
- What is your undying passion?

Everybody has something they can write about. Perhaps the best question you can ask yourself is: What are people always coming to me for? Relationship advice? If that's the case, you don't have to be a psychologist to write a book on relationships. You could do it in the style of an advice columnist, with questions and answers on various relationship topics. Or you could interview several professionals and create a book on the best relationship advice from the experts. There are many ways you can make a book credible through exhaustive research.

Are people always asking you for business advice? You can use a book to elevate your business credibility. Imagine you're soliciting a contract that could mean more lucrative jobs down the road. Maybe the potential client could raise your company to the next level, allowing you to expand and hire more people. The client must decide between you and another individual with exactly the same credentials and business experience. Your competitor leaves the interview saying, "Here's a copy of my brochure. It talks about some of the things we discussed." However, when your interview is finished, you say, "Here's a copy of my book. It talks about some of the things we discussed." Which candidate do you think the company will be inclined to hire?

You can use a book to elevate your business credibility.

The following book ideas are examples of finding a niche arising from your passion:

- Histories (write about your company, community, family, hobbies, etc.)

- Self-help books (if your company is a cleaning company, offer tips on how to get tough stains out of carpet; if you're a parent, write about how to get the most out of your kids, how to shop on a budget, etc.)

- Business and management advice (Dan Seidman's book *The Death of 20th Century Selling* is a hilarious look at 50 bad sales calls and how one can learn from them)

- Cookbooks (if your family and friends can't get enough of your cooking, you might be able to put together a best-selling cookbook)

- Inspiration (what can others learn from your overcoming a challenge? What have you done that can save others money and grief?)

Anyone can write a book, but it takes some thought to write a book that other people will want to read. Look into your own experiences and expertise to come up with an angle, and once you do, you may find there is more than one book inside you.

2
Charting Your Course

Now that you have an idea of what you want to write about, take the time to map out a plan. Whether you are going to publish the book yourself or pitch it to a publisher, you need to have an outline of your book. But first, you need to prepare a business plan, particularly if you are planning to self-publish. Think of it as starting a new business. You're investing hundreds of hours and perhaps years in developing your manuscript. You ought to have an idea of where you're going before you begin.

A Business Plan — Your Book's Map and Timeline

If you're not sure how to draft a business plan, refer to one of the many books on the subject, look for samples on the Internet, or you may find that there's a template available in your word-processing or office software (PowerPoint has some good ones). Self-Counsel Press's *Start and Run* series offers business plans for a range of home-based businesses, from operating a bed-and-breakfast business to running a landscape maintenance business. You can customize these plans according to your needs, but as you put a plan together, you'll need to ask yourself the following questions:

- What message do you want to send? What do you want readers to get out of your book?

If you're writing a book to make money or to become famous, perhaps you shouldn't be writing at all.

- What do you want the book to accomplish? If you're writing it to make money or to become famous, perhaps you shouldn't be writing at all. Who, besides you, will care? You need to have a broader purpose, something that will appeal to a range of people. You may want to advance knowledge in your field, eradicate illiteracy, inspire others to greatness, or teach people techniques for making their lives simpler.

- Related to your purpose, who is your audience? You could say, "everyone," but if your book is about football, is everyone a football fan? Is everyone going to be interested in your proven sales techniques? Is everyone going to want to read a romance novel? Think about who will be interested in your topic and write to those people. Find out as much as you can about them so you know how to catch and keep their interest. (See the section "It's about the Reader" in chapter 8.)

- How will you market this book? Don't fool yourself into thinking that people will automatically throw money at you because you've written a book. If you have a website, do people automatically access it? Are you plucking money off a tree because you have a web presence? Not likely. Just like websites, books have to earn their readership. Even if you place your book with a traditional publisher, if you, as the author, don't invest time and energy in marketing the book, it will disappear from the shelves faster than you can say "returns." The marketing section of your business plan should be specific and detailed. (See chapter 8 for more on marketing.) Include media opportunities, book signings, and always keep in mind who your target reader is.

- One of the most important topics, of course, is money. How are you going to come up with the financing? If you are self-publishing a well-designed, professional-looking book, you can count on needing roughly $10,000 — before you consider the costs of marketing, and leaving aside any thought of compensation for the time it will take you to write it. Design and layout, depending on the designer's hourly rate (and don't hire someone just because they're the cheapest), can range from $1,200 to $2,500 and up. Printing costs will depend on many factors (as you'll see in chapter 7), but for argument's sake, budget at least $5,000 for 1,000 books. If you need a lawyer to peruse potentially libelous material, add another $2,500. If you hire a professional editor, that will be another $2,500 (depending on the size of the book). Your biggest expense will be printing. Fortunately, all the expenses are not due at the same time. You might do what I did and max out credit cards, raid your savings account, and call in all favors from friends. Perhaps you qualify for a "business" loan. But bank on it costing you something.

- What's your timeline? Do you want to have your book available in time for some event? A trade show, maybe, or the start of the hockey season? The anniversary of a World War II battle or the founding of a local institution? If so, when do you need to have the manuscript ready for the publisher or printer in order to have finished books for that event? Get out your calendar and work back from there to create realistic timelines for finishing the manuscript. You need to factor in potential delays, other people's schedules, and family obligations. Always expect the unexpected when mapping a timeline. Of course, most of us are good at procrastinating. Having a due date, and secretly believing the project will be killed if it isn't ready by that date, will ensure you create a realistic schedule. (This is important even if you end up placing your book with a traditional publisher. In that case, missing a due date really *could* result in the project being killed, especially if you are a first-time author.)

Note that even if you're hoping to interest a traditional publisher in publishing your book, you must create a detailed marketing plan *as if* you were self-publishing. Don't expect the publisher to market your book (more on this in chapters 4 and 8). In fact, a good marketing plan can convince a publisher to accept a book.

Sample 2 shows an example of a business and marketing plan.

An Outline — Your Book's Résumé

After your business plan is developed, you should create an outline. The book's business plan will help you organize your time and stay focused on your purpose and audience, but your outline is your book's résumé. This is your sales letter, your first and last opportunity

SAMPLE BUSINESS AND MARKETING PLAN

Future Prospects — The Book

Future Prospects takes a behind-the-scenes look at the world of major junior hockey. Focusing on the players' perspective, this book looks at some of the unique aspects of major junior hockey, such as leaving home at a young age, juggling hockey and travel with school commitments, draft issues, and the influence coaches have on their careers and their lives.

Purpose

The reader gains an insider's view of what it's like to be a player, the challenges faced, and the lifelong camaraderie, as well as having a few chuckles over some really good stories.

The book helps potential future prospects and their parents learn what to expect if they ever have the opportunity to enter this world

Readers

- General hockey fans, particularly in Canada but also internationally
- Junior hockey enthusiasts
- Grassroots teams, players, coaches, parents
- Communities with direct ties to major junior hockey

Competition

- Other hockey books: there are few books on the market about major junior hockey and even fewer books that take a behind-the-scenes approach from the same perspective
- Hockey books written by more high-profile writers
- NHL-licensed products

Positioning

- Behind-the-scenes look at major junior hockey from the players' perspective
- Independently published — control over timing of release and ability to include sponsorship material at time of publishing

Communication Strategies

1. Junior Hockey Teams
   - Send review copies of book and excerpts from book to hockey organizations and tabloid publications directed at junior hockey (WHL, OHL, *Hockey's Future*)
   - Solicit sponsor to cover cost of printing and distribution to teams
   - Bulk purchase offer to teams
   - Book signings at key junior hockey arenas
   - Work other promotion ideas with Western Hockey League

2. Professional Hockey Teams
   - Solicit teams to carry book in their souvenir shops
   - Offer bulk purchase to teams for season ticket holders and special promotions — particularly those teams whose players are featured in the book
   - Offer excerpts to post on their websites or include in season ticket holders' newsletters

3. Seminars, Keynotes
   - Offer to speak at hockey banquets and functions and have books available for sale

4. Advertising
   - Place display ads in trade magazines or publications that offer the best advertising value — perhaps *The Hockey News*
   - Donate books to nonprofit organizations and teams to use for hospital visits, charity benefits, and children's organizations, particularly those that help kids with sports registration and equipment, such as KidSport

5. Specialty Advertising
   - Provide display posters of book cover to key retail/bookstore outlets, and use them at public appearances
   - Use postcards or bookmarks of the book cover for multipurpose mail-outs
   - Add the book cover to return address labels, letterhead, and other items that might help market the book

6. Book Clubs, Bookstores, Retail
   - Solicit a distributor that will get books into bookstores nationwide or internationally
   - Solicit book clubs and specialty retail shops (such as sporting goods stores)

7. Sell Direct to Associations, Corporations, and Niche Markets
   - International hockey leagues and associations (e.g., Hockey Canada or USA Hockey), sports travel clubs, media outlets
   - Offer bulk rates for their members to use as gifts, membership incentives, etc.

8. Schools
   - Speak to schools about the lifestyle of major junior hockey, perhaps taking a junior player with me

9. Media
   - Solicit media interviews — nationally and internationally — on an ongoing basis

- Position myself as the behind-the-scenes expert and develop a script regarding three points to address with a quick solution (e.g, *After years as a sports reporter and administrator, I've discovered three things that aspiring athletes need to know as they strive for a professional career: 1. It isn't always about skill. Attitude, will, and perseverance play a key role in helping kids make it. 2. They need to... 3. They need to...*)
- Pitch a radio/television treatment (including a brief description of 13 potential episodes) for 90-second segments that help future prospects reach their goals. These might include a short clip with a professional player talking about specific things he's learned and wished he knew beforehand, or clips of major junior players that focus on their unique lifestyle.
- Offer giveaway books to media for their listeners, readers, and viewers, particularly for the sports talk shows

Launch Strategies

- Schedule promotion for during junior hockey playoffs
- Send promotional copies to review media prior to the launch

Promotion Budget

- Get quotes for printing postcards or bookmarks
- Estimate postage for television pitch and other mail-outs
- Limit advertising costs to the ideal publication — *The Hockey News* — periodic advertisements @ $235 per issue
- Estimate courier costs for out-of-town bulk deliveries

Other Marketing

- Third-party marketing: Look for partnership opportunities that are win-win for both parties
- Focus on bulk sales and consignment distribution
- Solicit sponsor to cover the cost of book printing
- Look for out-of-town opportunities for book signings and schedule satellite sales or events around it

Pricing

- Set retail price and bulk purchase and discount prices
  For example:
  US$12.00/CDN$15.00 retail per book
  US$20.00/CDN$12.00 for 10-book purchase
  US$320.00/CDN$350.00 per box of 54
  US$2.46/CDN$3.00 per book for orders of 2,000+

Scheduling

- Regularly schedule time for prospecting bulk sales — perhaps two hours a day on an ongoing basis
- Develop a production timeline, working backward from the launch date:
  - September: Junior hockey playoffs
  - Books in hand: August 20
  - Ship from printer (1 week): August 13
  - Send to printer for production (6 weeks): July 1
  - Allow one week for delays or problems: June 24
  - Send manuscript to designer (2 weeks): June 10
  - Allow one week for delays or problems: June 3
  - Have designer work on front cover; solicit ISBN and CIP numbers: April
  - Write and edit manuscript (3 months):* Start March 1
  - Research and conduct interviews: November to March
  - Create outline and business/marketing plan: October

*Note: the length of time needed to write and edit will vary widely depending on the author, the subject, and the book length.

to get people interested in your book. Whether you are pitching your book to a traditional publisher, a distributor, booksellers, media, or even a high-profile person you'd like to interview, they will use the outline to base their decision whether or not to support you.

You'll want to start the outline with a catchy title. Coming up with the right name can be as onerous as writing the manuscript. The title should reflect what the book is about. It should be memorable, whether it achieves that by being witty, poignant, or dramatic. A simple title is best. If it's vague, boring, complex, or misrepresentative, it's not going to compel someone to read your proposal, let alone pick the finished book off the shelf.

Look at the titles of similar books for ideas. Take a hint from the daily newspapers. Headlines can tweak your creativity.

Like a press release, the overview should be written in inverted pyramid style, giving the most important information first and continuing on to the least important.

For more ideas, jot down words that pertain to your topic. For example, if your book is about football, words that might come to mind are gridiron, field, touchdown, field goal, quarterback, helmet, tackle, fumble.

Think about how you would define your book's message in one word. Look that word up in your thesaurus and see what other words could be used to coin a catchier phrase.

Use the industry terminology and the theme words and try to come up with a winning combination. Test your title ideas on family members, friends, and colleagues to find out which ones they like and why.

Besides a title, your outline should include the following:

1. A general overview of the project. This should be three to four carefully worded paragraphs describing the essence of your book. There is no room for vagueness. Like a press release, the overview should be written in inverted pyramid style, giving the most important information first and continuing on to the least important. The reader should get the substance of the story in the first paragraph, without having to read further. The overview may be the most important words you write — more important than the text of the book itself. This text sells your book. It is as important as the blurb on the back cover. In many cases, much of this text is used for the back cover.

2. A theme statement that describes what the reader will get out of your book. This will help a publisher determine if it should invest in your book. It also reinforces your purpose and gives interviewees a good understanding of what they're getting involved in.

3. Details of the research or interviews that you will be doing. This information adds credibility to your book. It shows that you are doing the work to ensure your material is accurate. These are the book's credentials. Some of the interviews may also be a selling feature of your book. If you are talking to celebrities and high-profile individuals, their involvement will lend merit to your book. For example, if you are writing about what you did to cope with or combat a medical problem, much of the material will be drawn

from your own experiences, but interviews with doctors and therapists who know the topic inside out will lend even more value to the information in your book.

4. A list of similar books currently on the market, with information on how your project is unique. If you haven't researched what's been published on your topic, how do you know someone else hasn't already written the same book? I suggest you visit the website of a major bookstore, such as Barnes & Noble, Chapters/Indigo, or Amazon. Using the book search, get as specific as you can with keywords that describe your book. See what pops up and take note of books that closely match yours. If you are writing about the social impact of an industry and the only books you can find are technical books, list a couple of the technical books and make a note of your findings. Before preparing the proposal for my book *Future Prospects*, I looked online for other books about major junior hockey, especially those that took a behind-the-scenes look. I found two books — period. The rest were team publications that didn't deal with the whole world of major junior hockey.

5. A description of your target audience. Your target audience is important to potential publishers. The size of the audience will indicate whether it's worth taking on the book. Publishers will also know if they have the expertise to reach the audience. If you're writing about sports, a literary publisher is unlikely to be interested in the book as its marketing apparatus will be aimed at the wrong readers and media. This also keeps you focused on targeting publishers and industries that reflect your reader.

6. A list of your credentials. What are your qualifications for writing this book? If it's a book about a health issue that has personally affected you, therein lies part of your expertise. If it's a topic in which you have no qualifications but on which you have done extensive research, you still have to have a reason for writing this book. If it's been your lifelong passion, say that. Describe your connection to the material.

7. If you're pitching the book idea to a traditional publisher, you should also include a well-thought-out marketing plan

When you look at *your* book's purpose, think about what readers will get out of it.

for reaching this target audience, information on the status of the manuscript (how much have you written and when will it be completed?), and an approximate page or word count.

Ron and Adrianna Edwards describe how important the outline is for your book:

> The outline will make or break the sale. In a few rare cases where a publisher knows the packagers and trusts them implicitly, a short, even vague, outline is all that is needed, but that is becoming extremely rare as publishers must pass every book idea through editorial and publishing committees. These are increasingly anonymous and bureaucratic, and the packager never gets the chance to present to these groups in person. That is why the outline is so critical. It has to sell your idea for you.

It's just as important when you self-publish. The outline becomes your marketing flyer in selling the media on interviewing you about your book, soliciting a distributor to carry your book in a bookstore, and even persuading a potential interviewee whom you want to include in your book. See Sample 3 for an example of an outline.

When Goldie Hawn was interviewed on CNN about her book *A Lotus Grows in the Mud,* she was asked why it wasn't a tell-all book about movie industry and the people in it. Her response: she looked at the book's purpose. The book was meant to be inspirational. She had a lot of interesting stories to tell, but each of those stories had a purpose for being told, a lesson people could take into their own lives. She positioned her book as a spiritual journey of a heart in search of enlightenment.

When you look at *your* book's purpose, think about what readers will get out of it. What will they learn? Will they be entertained? Will it help them overcome a challenge? Once you know your book's purpose, it's easier to plan when, where, and how to sell the story.

BOOK OUTLINE

Future Prospects

Major junior hockey is as close to professional hockey as you can get. Close-knit towns across the country define themselves by their major junior hockey team and take pride in players who go on to careers in the National Hockey League.

Future Prospects takes a behind-the-scenes look into the world of major junior hockey, focusing on some of the unique aspects players face, such as leaving home at a young age, juggling hockey and travel with school commitments, draft issues, and the influence coaches have on their careers and lives.

Players discuss the difficult adjustments they have to make, including the jump from minor hockey to major junior and what it's like to go back to junior after attending a professional hockey camp.

The reader gains an insider's view of what it's like to be a player, the challenges faced, and the lifelong camaraderie, as well as having a few chuckles over some really good stories.

The book helps potential future prospects and their parents learn what to expect if they ever have the opportunity to enter this world.

Interviews

Features interviews with Kelly Hrudey, Mike Modano, Jiri Fischer, Ron Robison, Andrew Ference, Ryan Getzlaf, Mike Egener, Doug MacLean, Jacques Lemaire, Ethan Moreau, Nigel Dawes, Mike Ricci, Richard Zednik, Patrice Brisebois, Alex Tanguay, Luc Robitaille, Mike Rathje, Braydon Coburn, and Jamie McLennan, to name a few.

What's on the Market?

- Lapp, Richard and Silas White. *Local Heroes: A History of the Western Hockey League.* Harbour Publishing (ISBN 1-55017-080-5), 1993.

- Lapp, Richard. *The Memorial Cup: Canada's National Junior Hockey Championship.* Harbour Publishing (ISBN 1-55017-170-4), 1997.

- Various team publications

Target Audience

- Hockey fans, players, and parents

Author's Qualifications

- Wrote, edited, and project managed over 25 books

- National Hockey League reporter for over 10 years

- Author and publisher of *Inside the NHL Dream* (ISBN 0-9730237-0-8) and *Positive Sports: Professional Athletes and Mentoring Youth* (ISBN 0-9730237-3-2)

- Author of *Self-Publishing 101,* published by Self-Counsel Press (2005)
- First woman to "headman" a football team and conference in Canada (president of the Calgary Colts Football Club; president of the Prairie Football Conference)
- Former public relations director, Edmonton Trappers Baseball Club
- Long-time major junior hockey supporter

3
Sculpting Your Book

A book is like a sculpture. An artist starts with a slab of stone and chips away, piece by piece, until an image starts to take shape. As the image emerges, the artist smoothes out the edges and uses different tools to carve intricate details. Writing is the same, using words instead of stone.

Get Organized

Before you start writing, it's usually a good idea to get organized. You've come up with an idea, thought about what you want to say, and done your research. Now you have a box full of papers — notes you've jotted down, ideas, research, and clippings. In your desk drawer are cassette tapes you've used to capture notes and interviews.

The first thing to do is organize the paperwork into topics. You might have 6 to 15 separate subjects, which would be quite broad. Each subject could be a separate chapter, or you might decide to break a general subject into smaller parts, or group two or three smaller subjects together in one chapter. Now you can scratch out a rough table of contents, jotting down subjects as chapter headings and discovering where you need to fill the gaps to round off the book.

If you are writing a novel, the process is similar, but you also need to organize all the book's characters, their relationship to the main subjects in the story, who they are, their background, physical characteristics, and when they come into the story.

Once you've organized the paperwork (which usually means having piles of paper all over your office or living room), you can set up an organization system that works for you. This might be a set of file folders, a binder, or some other method. This process is the key to creating your book. While the information may not have been gathered in sequence, and the chapters may not be written in sequence, you must have an idea of how they will all fit together in order for your book to flow smoothly.

Next, you might want to start transferring your information to your computer. Set up a folder for your book, and then a folder for the manuscript. Inside that second folder, you might create one file for the manuscript, separate files for each chapter, or separate folders for each chapter. (Eventually, you will have to merge all the chapters into one file, but at the beginning, it's often easier to work on smaller electronic chunks.) Now you can start entering information for each chapter as bullet notes. As you transcribe your tapes, slot the information into appropriate chapters you've created.

Now you're ready to sculpt your masterpiece. Go through each chapter to make sense of your notes. Start to rough out sentences, and move misplaced paragraphs to improve the flow. Ask yourself, is it important to leave this part in? Where do I need to add more information? (Unlike a slab of stone, which can only be made smaller, a slab of words can have material added.) Who can I interview to fill this gap in the text?

How the Pros Do It

Everyone will have a different method for writing and organizing a book. What may work for one person doesn't always work for another. I am the queen of cut and paste — physically. I cut up printouts with my material on it, arrange and rearrange the pieces, paste them together, and then arrange them electronically. Others may work better on the computer, without the physical aspect of the cut and paste. Here are some words of advice from successful authors on how they organize their work.

Audrey Bakewell is a power-skating coach who has helped shape the careers of some of the National Hockey League's biggest stars. To augment her clinics throughout North America and

Europe, she wrote *Get the Edge,* an instruction manual for her power-skating techniques:

> I just started putting ideas down on the paper. I tried to compile the book the same way as I teach, in progression, from basic to advanced, easy to difficult. The most challenging part was remembering all the skills that I teach because I tend to make up methods as I go.

Develop an outline, do the research, set a deadline, and write.

Stan Fischler is known as the Hockey Maven. He has written and co-written over 100 books, is a three-time New York Emmy Award winner for his work as an analyst on the New York Islanders and New Jersey Devils telecasts, and was named Centennial Historian of the City of New York by Mayor Rudy Giuliani. He is an NHL analyst for numerous media outlets and is the editor and publisher of *The Fischler Report.* His books have lined the shelves of many a hockey fan for years. He has written books with and about such notable stars as Kevin Lowe, Bobby Orr, Brad Park, Rod Gilbert, Derek Sanderson, and Don Cherry.

Fischler's manuscript development process varies:

> It depends if it's a book that I ghost. I ghosted Don Cherry's book. I taped the interviews and did that with Derek Sanderson, Brad Park, and Rod Gilbert. I taped and transcribed the interviews. I gather research, so I know as much as possible about the guy to add material that he might not have given me. Then I do a rough draft of the piece. I send it to the publisher and say, "Make any of the changes that you want to and we'll go from there." That's a pretty simple way of doing things, and it's worked. If it's a complicated book, like the encyclopedia that my wife Shirley and I have done, you have to have people to help you — research people.

Warren Redman, president of the Centre for Inner Balancing, says:

> I develop an outline of what I want to say, research the information that I need, give myself a deadline, and stare at the computer. That's the challenging part — seeing the blank screen. The best advice I ever got when I declared to an editor friend that I

was stuck was, "Just write — whatever it is, something will come out." The other hard part was going back and rewriting it.

Bruce Dowbiggin is a well-known columnist, broadcaster, and winner of two Gemini Awards as Canada's top sportscaster. To compile the text for his four books, he says:

> I use some material gleaned for the [Calgary] *Herald* and supply the rest myself. The most challenging part is keeping up your momentum over two, three years.

Tom Douglas has used a couple of different methods:

> In the case of *Some Sunny Day,* it became a game. My wife, Gail, challenged me to set down my memories about incidents that happened, and I would turn the short stories over to her one by one. When we had enough for a small book I started shopping around to traditional publishers, but nobody was interested. They said personal memoirs were a hard sell. But their rejection letters were encouraging and helpful, so we decided to go the self-publishing route.
>
> With *Canadian Spies,* it was a case of remembering a lot of the stories the French-Canadian vets told me in Brittany, plus researching. The most challenging part was reading three or four different accounts of an event where each of them had "facts" that contradicted the others. You have to decide whose opinion you're going to accept and then hope that you aren't perpetuating an error.
>
> I had a very bad case of the flu when I started researching *Spies* and could hardly hold my head up, let alone write research notes. So I got a small tape recorder and read into it the stuff I wanted to refer to for later transcription. It worked so well that I now do that regularly. It takes longer because I have to transcribe it (although I'm considering buying one of those devices that recognizes your voice and types your written word onto the computer). However, in transcribing, it fixes the important material in my mind for later reference.

Take Your Idea for a Test Drive

You might want to test the market for a book idea by publishing an article first. This is no easy task. You'll need to find a periodical with the right fit. A good start is to go to your local library and look through back issues of magazines to see what angle they take on their articles. You're looking for ideas on how to shape your material to fit their publication. If, for example, you're writing an article about the germination of flowers, I doubt *The Hockey News* or *Forbes* would be interested — unless your angle is NHL star Steve Yzerman's greenhouse techniques or the overall perspective of the United States' flower-growing industry, respectively.

If you're a contractor or tradesperson, find the magazines that pertain to your area of expertise. For example, if you are an underground services contractor, there are magazines that specialize in this field. Pitch story ideas to where you want to write, but make sure you know the publication first. It's extremely important to research some of their back issues to see what their focus is.

Look at the most recent publication and take note of the managing editor. That's typically who you would send your proposal to. You would not send a completed article, but rather a letter outlining what the article is about and perhaps including a compelling excerpt. This query letter is similar to your book outline. The managing editor will want to know what qualifies you to write this article, who you plan to interview to give it credibility, and what experience you have as a writer. If the editor is interested, he or she will ask you to send a completed article. When you're ready to send something, make sure you've thoroughly edited it first. Nothing kills a story faster than spelling and grammar errors, which leads nicely to my next point.

To Be Taken Seriously as a Writer, Take Your Writing Seriously

Spelling plus grammar equals professionalism. How many times have you opened a book and couldn't get past the introduction because of poor sentence construction and misspelled words? If you are going to write a book, take the time and effort to make it your best work or hire someone to help you (see the section "Finding a Ghostwriter or Editor" in this chapter).

Stock a basic library of reference books — and use them.

Imagine paying $150 for an Alicia Keys concert. She comes out, sings two songs off-key, then leaves the stage, thinking to herself, "That was good enough." You'd want your money back, and that's how a reader will feel about your book if you put little effort into the spelling and grammar.

To start with, invest in a good dictionary (minimum 1,500 pages) and a comparable thesaurus. If you plan on writing most of your material in American English, invest in *Webster's New World Dictionary*. If you are most comfortable in Canadian English, use one of the Canadian English dictionaries. Keep in mind that most magazine and book publishers use American English, even if the product is printed in Canada.

Buy a stylebook. Associated Press (AP) or Canadian Press (CP) styles are typically used by the newspaper industry, and *The Chicago Manual of Style* is commonly used in the book publishing industry. A stylebook will show you how to use punctuation properly; the correct way to write plurals, possessives, and titles; how to use quotations and dialogue; and how to avoid a host of writing faux pas. Any time you are unsure where to put a comma, how to use an em dash, or when to capitalize a title, look it up.

Yeah, I know what you're thinking. Why spend $80 on a dictionary or stylebook when you can just use the spellchecker on your computer? Well, lazy lawyers don't win cases, and lazy writers won't get read. Spellcheckers do not catch homonyms, words out of context, or singular words that should be plural, and they often flag grammatically correct sentences as incorrect.

Buy other types of reference books to help you hone your craft. Then use them. The following are just a few of the books in my collection:

- *Cambridge Biographical Dictionary*, general editor Magnus Magnusson (Cambridge University Press, 1990)

- *Dictionary of Problem Words and Expressions* (revised edition), Harry Shaw (McGraw-Hill, 1987, OOP)

- *The Everyday English Handbook*, Leonard Rosen (Doubleday, 1985)

- *National Textbook Company's Dictionary of American Slang and Colloquial Expressions*, Richard A. Spears (National Textbook Company, 1989) — because it's fun to flip through

- *Write Right!* Jan Venolia (Ten Speed Press, 2001)

Here are some simple tips to improve your writing:

1. Simplify your language. Don't use five words when one word will do. For example, instead of using "at this point in time," say "now."

2. A short word will often have more impact than a long word.

3. If a word is not essential, take it out.

4. Don't assume everyone knows your industry jargon or is impressed by foreign phrases and scientific words. If there is an everyday English equivalent, use it.

5. Be consistent. If you use American English, don't insert "our" in words like neighbour and colour — it's neighbor, color. Spell out symbols like %, and use either "percent" or "per cent" consistently. For numbers, it is common practice to spell out one to ten; use digits for anything over ten.

6. Check the spelling of titles, names, and companies. Sometimes we take things for granted. While writing one newspaper article, I assumed I spelled a name correctly, or, rather, used the proper initials: YMCA. I checked it throughout the article to make sure it was consistent. I sent in the story, satisfied it was correct. I was wrong. It should have been YWCA. A simple check against the brochure I had printed off the website would have saved me embarrassment and a tongue lashing from my editor.

7. Commas, dashes, quotation marks, apostrophes — when in doubt, look it up. One of the most common mistakes is using the wrong form of "its/it's." "Its" is possessive and means "something that belongs to it." "It's" means "it is." If you say "it is" every time you see it written as "it's," you're more likely to catch the error if you use it incorrectly.

8. Use language that engages the reader's senses — how did things smell, feel, sound, taste? What did they look like? Use action words to show what's happening. Get dramatic. Practice by noticing things around you — describe the contours of your cat's fur or how the calloused hands of your grandmother told the story of her life.

9. Write the way you would talk to a friend ... without the "ums" and "you knows."

See Appendix 2 for some editing exercises.

Editing — The "Seven Times" Rule

Use the "seven times" rule of editing. This means you'll read your manuscript at least seven times. Read it twice onscreen, making changes as you go. Print off a copy and you'll notice smaller errors jumping off the page at you. For example, you'll notice you missed the "d" in "and." This is the kind of thing you'll overlook on the screen. Go through the electronic version again, inputting the changes from your hard copy. Read it again onscreen. Print it off again and go through the hard copy. Then read it onscreen while inputting the new changes. Glance over it once more. Your manuscript will now be nearing perfection.

Don't do all these steps in one shot. In fact, after the first couple of edits it's good to walk away from the manuscript for a while — even a day — before diving back in. In one of the latter onscreen edits, read sentences aloud. This will help you catch errors and also give you a sense of how well your writing flows.

If by the time the book comes off the press you feel nauseous at the thought of reading it again, you'll know you've done a good job of editing.

Finding a Ghostwriter or Editor

You've decided you absolutely have to write a book, but you can't do it on your own. You need help. You can hire someone to help you write the best book possible. This could be a ghostwriter, who will write the manuscript for you, or an editor, who will work with you to improve the manuscript you've already written. This person would worry about the style issues, spelling, grammar, and all those things that are time-consuming to look up. Sometimes your manuscript might require a bit of both.

Ghostwriters

Sometimes a person will come up with a great idea for a book, but due to work or family commitments, he or she doesn't have time to write it. Other people might be uncomfortable with the task of writing. They may be unable to fully develop their thoughts on paper. In cases like this, who are they going to call? A ghostwriter!

Jill Lublin, co-author of *Guerrilla Publicity* and *Networking Magic*, reveals her opinions about the value of ghostwriters:

> I compiled the text for my books by hiring a ghostwriter. The problem that most people have is that they keep saying they want to write a book, and three years later I meet them, and they still haven't written their book. I recommend to people to find a ghostwriter, find an editor, find a support team for your writing project, and hand it over — delegate it. How I completed the text was really finding a great ghostwriter. The challenging thing about this was finding the right partner — the person who could write correctly. Who was the best match for me? Who captured my thoughts in a really positive way? I think it's really important to find a person who you can resonate with, who gets your voice properly, and who gets who you are, the gist of you. I actually had to go through a few writers to find that. Gratefully, I found one.

Finding the right ghostwriter can be challenging. You might need to interview several writers to find your best match.

Claudia Suzanne, who wrote, edited, and ghosted over 50 books, says in her article "The Good Life of Ghostwriting" (available online at the *WritersWeekly* website) that book industry insiders estimate 50 percent or more of all traditionally published books are worked on by a ghostwriter, book doctor, or line editor. The statistics are much higher in self-publishing.

A ghostwriter will listen to the author's life story, business techniques, lifestyle tips, or whatever, and write it all down — in the author's own voice. It is the author's material, his or her name will be on the cover, so the finished product should give the impression that he or she wrote it. After all, the contents are often the author's life's work.

Because the subject matter can be so personal, authors hiring ghostwriters will want to be totally comfortable with the people they hire. They need to be convinced that the ghostwriter understands their purpose and their message. If necessary, the ghostwriter should have a full understanding of the terminology used in the author's industry.

Responsibilities of Authors and Ghostwriters

The author

- Supplies the ideas, plan, or theory; the stories; and the outline
- Cooperates with the ghostwriter so he or she can meet the deadline
- Pays the ghostwriter

The ghostwriter

- Needs no byline (i.e., credit as the book's author) because the material belongs to the author
- Doesn't change the material to reflect his or her own style — even if a byline is offered
- Maintains the author's voice so the reader will recognize the material as the author's, not the ghostwriter's
- Leaves the characters, plot, and ending alone
- Provides a readable manuscript that is well edited

Note: The book belongs to the author — not the ghostwriter.

To find a ghostwriter, ask around in your networking circles, ask other authors who have used one, and check for contacts online and through writing associations.

Editors

If you feel comfortable with the idea of writing down your ideas or memories, you will still want to have someone help you polish your manuscript. This is where an editor comes in. According to the Editors' Association of Canada (EAC), there are several different types of editing, including the following jobs that may be of interest to self-publishers:

- Substantive/structural editing (clarifying or reorganizing a manuscript for content and structure)
- Stylistic editing (clarifying meaning, eliminating jargon, polishing language, and other non-mechanical line-by-line editing)

- Copy editing (editing for grammar, usage, spelling, punctuation, and other mechanics of style; checking for consistency; placing artwork; editing tables, figures, and lists)

- Fact checking (checking accuracy of facts and quotes by referring to original sources used by the author or to other reference sources)

- Proofreading (checking proofs of formatted, edited material for errors in design and for minor mechanical errors in copy, such as spelling mistakes or small deviations from style sheet)

(This information is taken from the EAC Standard Freelance Editorial Agreement. For further information, see the EAC website, <www.editors.ca>.)

If you decide to hire an editor, you should follow the same process as you would in finding a ghostwriter. Be sure you feel comfortable with the person and that he or she understands your purpose and message. The editor you choose should be able to follow your guidelines. You determine the voice (passive or active), style (AP, CP, *Chicago Manual,* or other), and language (American or Canadian English) before you begin. The editor's job is to point out places where you are inconsistent in spelling or style, where your writing is unclear or awkward, and where you have made errors, whether these are spelling or grammar mistakes, or errors in fact. It's impossible for a manuscript to be absolutely perfect, but if you are meticulous in the editing process, it will be close to perfect.

If you hire an editor who doesn't understand your industry, he or she may question every aspect of your manuscript. This could be good or bad. For example, if you're writing a book on sales, you may be aiming your book specifically at experienced salespeople. That means you will be using generally recognized sales terminology. If an editor comes in and questions this terminology and doesn't understand the context of your chapters, you might decide instead to hire an editor who understands sales. On the other hand, if you are writing for people who want to learn about sales, they may not be familiar with the industry's terminology. In that case, an editor who questions the terminology and context may be pointing out areas where your readers will also have problems understanding what you are saying.

Depending on the content of your manuscript, you may want someone to check it for plagiarism or for material that might be construed as libelous. An editor may be able to do this, but if you think your book will be considered controversial, get a lawyer to vet it prior to publication.

Writing Is 99 Percent Perspiration

I receive many calls from people who want to know how to become a writer. Most of them don't like the answer. I tell them it is like wanting to become an actor. You have to study acting, act in amateur theater (without pay), go through the cattle calls, wait tables, usher in movie theaters — and hope to meet the people who can give you the big break.

Unless one of your parents owns a newspaper or you are extremely lucky, chances are it will take years of sweat and labor to get one thing published, and then it will take more work to get paid. You learn in a hurry that placing a book with a traditional publisher is as unlikely as getting onstage (or onscreen) with Keanu Reeves or Angelina Jolie in your first gig.

4

Dispelling the Myths about Publishing

When it comes to traditional publishing, there are many misconceptions: you'll become rich overnight, your books will always get into a bookstore, the publisher will invest large amounts of money to market your book — the list goes on.

Stan Fischler knows a little about this after writing and co-writing over 100 books for traditional publishers. What does he see as the biggest misconception about traditional publishing? "That authors can make a lot of money easily," says Fischler. "It's very difficult to make a buck unless you hit it good. I was lucky with the Bobby Orr book. It was 'right guy, right place, right time,' and it helped us build our house in the country. He was the hottest thing in hockey. We hit number one on the bestseller list in Boston. That doesn't happen that often."

Warren Redman agrees about the misconception: "Authors think that it's easy, and it makes you lots of money."

A publicist for a publisher that produces 30 to 50 titles annually says the biggest misconception she comes across is the author's expectations of success for a published book. Authors often hear enthusiastic sales projections from their agents and publishers, but when it comes time to market and promote the book, they're often disappointed with lackluster results. It's a tough industry, one in

Publishing Facts

The Association of American Publishers stated that book sales totaled US$23.7 billion in 2004. R.R. Bowker, North America's main source of information on books and publishing, reported in 2004 that there were over 2.8 million titles in print in the United States. Small and self-publishers accounted for 78 percent of the titles published, according to the Publisher's Marketing Association (PMA) (from the Para Publishing website, <www.parapub.com/statistics>).

The Association of American Publishers also said that in 2002, *half* the books printed and shipped to booksellers were returned to the publisher to be remaindered or destroyed. Half! (From <www.IanPercy.com>.)

Statistics Canada reported that in 2000–01, 627 publishers in Canada produced 15,744 titles, reprinted 12,053 titles, and produced over CDN$2.4 billion worth of revenue. However, only 56.4 percent of those publishers made a profit. The publishers Statistics Canada surveyed were those that select and edit works, enter into a contract agreement with an author or copyright holder, and market books, while bearing the associated costs — not the self-publishers whose books are also in bookstores.

Statistics Canada says books generated a pretax profit of CDN$167.8 million in 2000. Foreign-controlled firms accounted for CDN$82.8 million of that. Export book sales grew at twice the rate of sales of Canadian books.

The Publishers Marketing Association and the Book Industry Study Group released the report *The Rest of Us 2003: An Update of the 1998 Report on America's Independent, Smaller Book Publishers.* They discovered that independent and smaller publishers reach annual sales of between US$29.4 billion and US$34.3 billion. What is interesting is that this figure is between 10 percent and 27 percent higher than what was reported for the entire publishing industry. These types of studies prove that independent publishers are more important to the publishing industry than most people realize. Financial troubles have significantly stunted the unit growth of the larger book publishers, but smaller and medium-sized publishers are growing significantly.

Even with e-books entering the marketplace, various statistics have shown that the majority of individuals still prefer a physical publication. Xlibris stopped producing e-books in October 2003 because it discovered less than half a percent of books were being sold in that format. It was also receiving inquiries from people asking how they could print out their e-book, thus defeating the purpose of that medium.

According to the Department of Canadian Heritage, <www.pch.gc.ca>, there were more than 22,000 writers working in Canada in 2002. If you take a look at the number of writers working in your own neighborhood, this figure seems drastically low.

Here are other interesting facts about the publishing industry from the Para Publishing website, <www.parapub.com/statistics>:

- The Book Industry Study Group divulged that large chain stores account for 24.6 percent of book purchases, while book clubs sell 17.7 percent, smaller chains and independent stores sell 15.2 percent, and 5.4 percent are sold on the Internet.

- *Publishers Weekly* stated that women buy more books than men — to the tune of 68 percent of all books. Women also like to shop more in discount stores, while men like to shop in chain stores. Of books that are read, 53 percent are fiction and 43 percent nonfiction, and 64 percent of book buyers say the bestseller list is not important.

- A survey and special report produced in 1998 by Brenner Information Group shows that of the independent publishers polled, 54 percent were male, 42 percent were female, and 3 percent wouldn't say. The most popular business structure of an independent publisher is a sole proprietorship. Most (60 percent overall: 65 percent males, 76 percent females) operate from a home office. They publish an average seven titles each (four times as much nonfiction as fiction), and in 1997 they earned an average of US$420,000.

- The Brenner Group also says the typical independent publisher works an average of 50 hours per week, and over 80 percent have no pension or retirement program.

- A 2003 survey conducted by Tom Woll of Cross River Publishing Consultants revealed that 73,000 smaller and newer publishers earned US$29.4 billion in gross revenue. Although, 70 percent of those publishers with one to ten books in print earned less than US$100,000. Woll also confirmed that smaller publishers are *not* represented in traditional industry figures.

which few people achieve the financial status or acclaim they desire from peers and colleagues.

There is a misconception that a book published by a traditional publisher will automatically sit on a bookstore shelf. Books do not always get into bookstores — just ask any smaller publishing house. Booksellers peruse publishers' and distributors' catalogs and choose the titles they think they can sell. They aren't necessarily going to carry every new book.

Another misconception is that a traditional publisher will automatically market and promote your book. It is *crucial* for authors to be involved in the marketing process. After all, it's the author's product. The media is not interested in speaking to marketing directors or publicists about the book. Books are most successful when all parties involved pool their resources and work together to effectively market the book.

But before your book sells well or poorly, before it is promoted and marketed or not, you have to get a publisher to accept it. That may be the most difficult step of all. In fact, it might be easier to get an invitation to the Vatican than to interest a publisher in taking on your book.

Why It's Easier to Get an Audience with the Pope

Self-Counsel Press, the company that produced this book, publishes 30 books each year, but will receive over 2,500 pitches. Larger publishing firms will receive many thousand submissions and publish less than one percent of them. This is the reason it's so difficult to place your book with a traditional publisher — and why self-publishing is a viable option.

If you plan to pitch to a traditional publisher, you must have a great outline. Your outline maps out your vision, spells out what makes the book special, and describes the reader or market you are targeting (see Sample 3 in chapter 2).

Before you start sending your outline to publishers, you need to research who is publishing books in the subject area you are writing about. Don't waste time and money by sending out pitches to every publisher you can find. Go online and visit publishers' websites. See what types of books they are publishing and if your book fits in with their list.

Most of the time, publishers will post manuscript submission requirements. If they say they don't want to see unsolicited manuscripts, don't send your entire manuscript — it won't get read! Most publishers will request that you send an outline, and possibly a sample chapter, by mail only. Very rarely will they accept solicitations online. Know what they want before you send it.

The bottom line: publishers want manuscripts that fit their market niche and their vision.

Too often, a writer labors over a manuscript for months, even years, with a specific publisher in mind without checking the publisher's website or catalog to see what the company actually publishes. When the writer receives a rejection slip, he or she solicits other publishers, sending full manuscripts, with the same result. After several hundred dollars' worth of photocopies and postage, the author is crushed. But don't despair — there is a good chance all of us went through the same expensive education.

The bottom line: publishers want manuscripts that fit their market niche and their vision. They want writers who can deliver those manuscripts, who are qualified and knowledgeable, and who can give them what they want.

When you have determined a shortlist of publishers who might be interested in your book idea, write a clear, concise cover letter to accompany your submission (see Sample 4). This letter is almost as important as your outline. If the first paragraph of your letter or outline doesn't grab the publisher's attention, your project will hit the bin with the rest of the 9,750 rejects.

Warren Redman has published 14 books, so he has had a lot of practice with submissions and rejections:

> I have had different experiences — from making a pitch to publishers and getting rejections (many) and acceptances (a few), and being asked by a publisher to write a couple of books (after they already published one of mine). Generally, it's a long, tough journey unless you happen to meet the right person or are lucky enough to pitch something that is exactly what the publisher happens to be looking for at that time.

SAMPLE 4
SAMPLE PITCH TO TRADITIONAL PUBLISHER

August 15, 20--

R.N. Editor
All-Star Publishing
111 First Place Road
New York, NY 11110

Dear Ms. Editor:

I'm contacting you because I noticed your firm published *Winning the Grey Cup: A History of the Canadian Football League.*

I have written a book about the lifestyle of the Canadian Football League (CFL) from the players' perspective. There is nothing like this on the market. I've published a similar book on the National Hockey League and major junior hockey (*Inside the NHL Dream* 2002 ISBN 0-9730237-0-8 and *Future Prospects* 2004 ISBN 0-9730237-4-0). *Inside the NHL Dream* has received rave reviews from readers both inside and outside the NHL fraternity.

I have met with CFL alumni _____, to go over the topics to be discussed. I think this book is long overdue. It will look at what the players' lives are actually like, and I'll be interviewing both current and former players.

I have written, edited, ghostwritten, and published over 25 books for both royalty and self-publishers. My background in football spans over 18 years as an administrator in junior football, with very close ties to the CFL. Many former junior players I've been associated with have gone on to professional careers. I was the first woman to "headman" a football conference in Canada as president of the Prairie Football Conference. I also spent three years at the helm of the Calgary Colts and served as an executive on the Canadian Junior Football League. I currently sit on the City of Calgary Sports Policy Steering Committee.

I also have a strong marketing/public relations/sales/event planning background with an "out of the box" style of thinking, which will come in handy when marketing this book.

I'm hoping All-Star Publishing will accept this book for publication, and I look forward to your positive reply.

Sincerely,

Debbie Elicksen

Audrey Bakewell agrees:

> The first publisher I met was at Peter Gzowski's book release. A colleague tried to make a deal for me with the publisher, but they later rejected me. I was at an NHL game and another colleague suggested I approach his publisher. They immediately took on the project.

Many books we now view as classics had an even longer road to publication. Richard Bach's *Jonathan Livingston Seagull* was rejected 26 times before the 27th publisher took a chance on a book for adults that told the story of talking, philosophizing seagulls. Margaret Mitchell's *Gone with the Wind* was turned down at least 25 times. Hans Christian Andersen was told his stories were unsuitable for children. Herman Melville, author of *Moby-Dick*, nearly gave up after numerous failures. A San Francisco daily newspaper fired Rudyard Kipling as a reporter because it said he couldn't use the English language.

Tom Douglas, who gained a traditional publisher after he self-published his first book, laughs:

> I have to tell you that I got a kick out of the [outline for *Self-Publishing 101*] where it says, "Why It's Easier to Get an Audience with the Pope." Gail and I, in fact, had a private audience with the Pope, which I arranged on a trip with the Veterans Affairs minister because he and his wife were Catholic, and part of our trip included a stop in Rome for the 40th anniversary of its liberation.

Jill Lublin might have had an easier time getting an audience in the Vatican:

> It took me about a year and a half to land the traditional publishing contract. It was probably a three-year process in total. The thing about the experience was, it felt very long to me. Once you're ready to write a book, you just want to get the book written. That was a little bit hard — just the waiting and waiting to say whether they wanted it or whether they liked it, whether they would accept it. For instance, we were at a major publisher. We went four rounds in the publishing world. Four

rounds through their editorial board and then they said no to me. Why they said no, I still don't know. That probably took another four to six months to just go through that process with that major publisher and then we ended up having to start from ground zero. Things like that were frustrating.

That said, a brand new author will occasionally get a publishing contract from the first pitch he or she sends out, and there are some lucky authors who didn't even have to make a pitch for their first book. A publisher approached Bruce Dowbiggin for his first book. Since then, he's had the same publisher, and a handful of others have approached him.

Stan Fischler had a similar experience:

The very first book I did was a biography on Gordie Howe. They came to me to say they wanted to do a hockey book on the best player in the world. I said that was Gordie Howe. The next book was *Bobby Orr and the Big Bad Bruins.* Bobby Orr happened to be the hottest guy in hockey. Then I ghosted the Derek Sanderson book. I proposed that one. Some of them I proposed. Some of them, they came to me.

Timing is everything. Sometimes the right pitch at the right time will be accepted with ease. It may only take a phone call.

At other times, what seems to be a brilliant book idea turns out to be a bust. In the spring of 2004, the Calgary Flames were the hottest team in sports, making a legitimate run for the Stanley Cup final after nearly a decade of missing the playoffs. Stan Fischler and I planned to co-write a book on the team's Cinderella season. We had an interested publisher and discussed the book's angle, marketing, and even money. Before the publisher sent out a contract, the Flames lost game seven of the Stanley Cup final to Tampa Bay, and the publisher opted out of the book project. While it was a good story, it would have made a better story if they had won. As it turned out, with the 2004–05 NHL season cancelled due to a collective bargaining impasse, it may have been a blessing for the publisher that the book did not go ahead. By the fall of 2004, the Flames' Cinderella season was nearly forgotten, and hockey books were thrown to the wayside until season play could be resumed.

Any time you pitch to a publisher, always remember it's not about you. The publisher wants to know if your idea is viable to the reader. It's all about sales, and the book has to mesh with the publisher's vision and list. A company that usually publishes children's picture books is unlikely to take on a statistical history of the National Football League, unless it's done in a simple format appealing to kids. The publisher's contacts, expertise, and vision are focused on children and what captures their attention. The amount of time, energy, and money the publisher would expend trying to figure out how to sell a statistical book on the NFL would eliminate any potential profit.

Here are some tips to keep in mind:

- Publishers will read few unsolicited manuscripts, if any.

- Publishers are driven by their vision, not yours.

- Publishers have their own opinion of what books will help them realize their vision.

- Only ideas decided on by the editor and publisher get published.

- A publisher might seek out an average writer who is an expert in a subject area.

- Sometimes another writer is assigned a good unsolicited idea.

Agents

The function of a literary agent is three-fold: find a publisher, negotiate the contract, and help the writer develop his or her manuscript.

An agent is a money manager. When he or she sells a proposal to a publisher, the agent receives money from the publisher, subtracts commission, and then forwards the remainder to the author.

Finding an agent is even more difficult than finding a publisher. Like publishers, agents reject 98 percent of the book proposals they receive. Why? Thanks to the consolidation of some of the larger firms, only a handful of publishers offer advances large enough to make the commission attractive for an agent.

To find an agent, you have to be as diligent as you would be looking for a publisher. Start by looking at the acknowledgment pages of books similar to yours to see if an agent is credited. If so,

Before you approach an agent, research the types of books he or she specializes in.

try and find him or her via phone listings. You may also track down agents through personal referrals from other writers or author testimonials at writing conferences.

The Association of Authors' Representatives is a nonprofit organization that provides a listing of literary and dramatic agents in the United States. Check its website, <www.aar-online.org>, for any listed agents in your area, but don't hold your breath. They are extremely difficult to find.

Once you have identified an agent or two who specialize in the type of book you have written, approach them as you would a publisher, with a letter and outline. Your query letter must entice an agent to read your outline. You must be able to accurately convince the agent about the importance and uniqueness of your book and why you should be the one writing it.

Writer Beware — Agent Scams

Reputable agents do not require fees up front. They receive a commission from the publisher's advance on royalties and/or revenue from book or rights sales. This is why agents are careful about the projects they take on. They have to be convinced of their marketability. If an agent pressures an author to pay any charges — even a photocopy charge — before the author's manuscript is sold to a publisher, it is inappropriate.

There are numerous individuals posing as agents who charge editing or reading fees before they decide to "accept" a manuscript. This is how they make their money — preying on the naive and vulnerable author.

It happened to me. I was just dipping my toe into writing as a possible profession. I had tons of ideas. I spent long hours researching one project. There were books published on the same topic, but not from quite the same angle. I was convinced it was a great idea. Serious about my writing, I was regularly purchasing *Writer's Digest* to augment my collection of writing reference books. In one issue I saw an advertisement under the "Literary Agents" heading and decided to respond. The ad said, "Experienced agency seeks writers; new writers welcome." It also listed two "recent" titles. After I responded to the ad, I received a phone call. They were more than happy to look at the manuscript and told me to send it with my check for US$75. At the time, that was a lot of money for me, but I paid it. Many months passed. When I called the agency to follow up, their response was, "What manuscript?" They finally uncovered it and offered to send it back with their editorial comments. I realized I had been ripped off long before I received the manuscript in the mail with a few chicken scratches on the pages.

Stan Fischler had a similar experience with an agent:

> I didn't have an agent for a long time. I did know a guy who was a hockey fan and an agent. We became friendly, and he knew I wanted to do a book. He pitched the idea to the publisher. They liked it, and it did fabulously well. This book did six or seven printings. Unfortunately, the way it worked then, the royalties went from the publisher to the agent. He stole a lot of money from me, and then wound up in another part of the country. I don't know how many hundreds of thousands of dollars we got screwed out of. It happened so many years ago. It's like when somebody steals your car. It's bad luck and you do your best to recoup from it. Before I used this agent and after I used him, I did have a dear friend who was a lawyer. I've used him to do my contracts on the books. I've since gotten another agent.

The Role of an Agent

Ron Edwards points out that most traditional publishers do not accept unsolicited manuscripts:

> The few that do [will] throw them into the slush pile to be reviewed by the most junior person. Chances of being published over the transom (unsolicited) are extremely rare. Agents have the ear of publishers, and the greater their experience, the more knowledgeable they are and the bigger their reputations. Publishers listen to agents.
>
> Literary agents do not take on new authors unless they are convinced they have something special that they can sell to publishers. It is a big sales job to convince an agent to take you on as a new

author. Also, as with publishers, agents do not want you if you are too "unique." They still have to sell you to the traditional publishers, who are a pretty conservative bunch and rely on the tried and true. They rarely stray outside their tiny circle. We have all heard the horror stories of masterpieces like *Moby-Dick* going unpublished for years. How many great books have died unpublished because traditional publishers were too insular to see the potential? Countless!

An agent will help open the door, but there *are* publishing houses that have published unrepresented authors. It never hurts to have an agent, but with most reputable agents not accepting new clients, it's a bit of a catch-22.

If you are lucky enough to land an agent, it's best to have your manuscript thoroughly edited before the agent asks to receive it. You want to make a good impression. Why would you send an unedited manuscript to the person who could make or break your chances of getting published?

Book Packagers

What is a book packager? Ron and Adrianna Edwards have packaged dozens of complete books and have been involved, in one form or another from proofreading through editing, in several hundred more. They explain:

> A book packager — or producer, as they prefer to be called — is a publisher without a warehouse and sales force. In other words, a packager does everything a publisher does except market and sell the book. In general, a packager will put together a team — from author to illustrator, editors, typesetters, and designers — to produce the finished book. Sometimes the packager will even arrange the printing. One crucial difference between publisher and packager is that the publisher can buy [a certain] number of books [from the packager] at a set unit price, and there are no returns.

This is in contrast to the publisher's relationship with bookstores, which buy books but are able to return them if they don't sell. So, the risk is greater for the publisher, but they can control costs better and stand to make better profits.

Most packagers function as literary agents in that they are selling a book idea to a publisher, usually with an author (and team) attached. The difference is that the packager has a personal stake in the project and oversees it from beginning to end, whereas an agent tends to negotiate the best advance and royalty for the author (less his or her own 10 or 15 percent fee) and walk away. Only a few agents get involved in the editorial and creative process. In Canada, the book publishing margins are so small that agents cannot afford to invest the time to baby the book along. That does happen in the United States from time to time on larger projects, but even there, it is rare. In short, literary agents deal in authors, while packagers deal in ideas.

The packager generally sells the book idea to the publisher via initial query. Once packagers get a green light, they crunch numbers. Assuming this all works out, the packager then puts together a team to produce a finished product. After a while, packagers develop a reputation with certain publishers and often a phone call is all that is needed. But with newbies starting out or packagers approaching new, unknown publishers, a full book proposal is needed. These used to be extensive, but as no one has the time to read 25 or more pages, the proposal should sum up the project in three or four pages. It is essential to be able to describe the book in a sentence or two, include a proposed table of contents with chapter titles, and describe other aspects of the book. Then outline the competition (and don't bother saying "This is unique," because they've all seen that before) and state how this book is different. The proposal should also include information about target audience and so on.

Contracts and Advances

If you are one of the lucky few who successfully lands a conventional publishing contract, particularly one that involves an advance on royalties, you might be wise to talk to a lawyer. Most publishers are flexible in their contracts, but it's up to the author to understand the contract before it is signed.

Stan Fischler emphasizes, "You have to have a lawyer to scrutinize the contract because there are things that could hurt you that you may not be aware of and only a lawyer would know. The lawyer doesn't have to specialize in publishing." He or she could specialize in contract law. Lawyers look for the fine print in contracts that most people miss. This fine print could cause a person much grief down the road.

Jill Lublin concurs — "The advice I would give someone is, don't negotiate the publishing contract yourself" — as do Ron and Adrianna Edwards:

> Most contracts appear to be written in Klingon, so get a Klingon to translate. A good lawyer is essential. Remember, there is no such thing as a "standard" contract. Everything is negotiable. On the other hand, try not to be such a pain in the ass that you are more trouble than you are worth. Don't ask for the moon, but don't give it away either. Most authors, especially new ones, are only too eager to give away the right of first refusal to the publisher (i.e., you agree to give the publisher first dibs on your next book). This can be a grave mistake, particularly if your book is a hit. Your next book will be tied up with that publisher.

A publishing contract may include clauses on some or all of the following points:

- *General publishing rights.* See the section "Rights and Copyright" in this chapter.

- *Manuscript delivery guidelines and schedule.* This sets out when the publisher expects to receive the manuscript.

- *Copyright terms.* Do you, the author, own the copyright or will it be in the publisher's name?

- *Assignment of royalties and payment schedule.* This sets out when and how much you get paid. The clause should also include information on when you will receive royalty statements, which indicate how many books you have sold and how much money the publisher owes you. Make a note of this date and follow up if you don't hear from your publisher within a reasonable time after that.

- *Subsidiary rights.* What happens if someone wants to republish the book in another format or country or offers a movie/television deal? Often the publisher will negotiate these deals and take a percentage of the payment. This clause sets out how much that percentage is. If you want to look after selling subsidiary rights yourself, you'll need to negotiate that.

Become familiar with the language of publishing contracts so that you understand what you are signing.

- *Translation rights*. Will your book be of interest to foreign language markets? Publishers might pay for the right to translate it into Spanish, French, or other languages. As with subsidiary rights, you need to decide whether you or the publisher will negotiate these deals and how you will split the payments.

- *Special sales*. This could cover sales to Wal-Mart and other bulk purchase ventures or to mail-order book clubs. These markets buy large numbers of books at a reduced price. As a result, you generally receive a lower royalty on these sales because the publisher is receiving less money for them. If you think you could arrange these sales yourself, you can have special sales taken out of the contract.

- *Merchandising rights*. If your book becomes a phenomenon like the *Harry Potter* series, who holds the rights for merchandising — creating and selling action figures, T-shirts, and other paraphernalia? How will revenues from merchandising be split?

- *Termination details*. How do you get out of a contract if it isn't working?

If you are co-writing a manuscript, it's especially important to hire a lawyer to peruse the contract or to draw up a collaboration agreement. This will clear up any discrepancies and ensure each author receives a fair share of any advance that is paid and of royalty payments after the book is published.

Don't sign a contract that will end up leaving a bad taste in your mouth. As Tom Douglas says:

> We're all so thrilled and eager when the first contract comes in that we sign away everything. Any contract I've seen is so loaded in favor of the publisher and against the writer that it's almost laughable. It's like the old expression about the Golden Rule: "Them that has the gold makes the rules." The problem is that for every one of us who might balk and say, "I'm not signing that!" there are 20

people lined up behind us ready to do whatever it takes to get published.

Rights and Copyright

What is copyright? According to *Webster's Dictionary*, it is "the exclusive legal right to reproduce, publish, and sell the matter and form ... of a literary ... work." This means that only you have the right to publish or allow someone else to publish your work.

From the moment your original manuscript exists in a physical form (i.e., in a computer file or handwritten into a notebook), you automatically hold the copyright on your material. In years past, writers were advised to mail a copy of their manuscripts to themselves and leave the mailing envelope sealed in order to prove they had copyright. This is not necessary. You can register copyright with the US Copyright Office, <www.copyright.gov>, or the Canadian Intellectual Property Office, <www.cipo.gc.ca>, but even this is not required for legal protection of your copyright.

Owning the copyright gives you, and you alone, the right to reproduce (in whole or in part), distribute, promote, and display the material. Nobody else can exercise any of these rights without your permission until the copyright expires — which happens 70 years after your death (50 years after death in Canada).

When you place your book with a publisher, you are agreeing to license that publisher to reproduce, promote, display, and distribute that literary work for a stated period of time — in other words, you're lending your rights to the publisher. In return for this privilege, the publisher pays you royalties on every copy of the book it sells.

Publishing contracts often contain clauses authorizing the publisher to arrange sales of subsidiary rights (e.g., sales to foreign publishers, translation to other languages, motion-picture rights, sales to book clubs or other special markets, or sales of excerpts). When a publisher sells these rights, it pays the author a certain percentage of the revenue from the sales. The percentage is stipulated in the contract. Before you sign the contract, you can try to negotiate a higher percentage of the revenue from sales of these rights, or you can refuse to give the publisher permission to handle these rights. In that case, you can sell them yourself or hire an agent to do it for you.

One of the most important items to look out for in a contract is the reversion clause, which states whether the publishing rights revert back to you when the book goes out of print or after a set period of time. The last thing you want to do is sign over your work with a no-reversion clause. Generally, books have a limited shelf life. Unless it's in continuous high demand, a book usually stays in the booksellers' systems for no more than one or two years. Unsold books are sent back to the publisher. There are times an author may want to republish the book after it's been taken off the shelf. This is the reason you need the rights reverted. A publishing contract with no reversion clause forbids you to reprint your own work.

Advances

An advance (or, more correctly, an advance against royalties) is a sum of money a publisher pays an author before a book is published. Often it is paid in two or more installments — one when the author signs the contract, another when the manuscript is delivered to the publisher, and additional installments at different steps of the process.

In order to understand how a publishing advance works, you need to understand how the bookselling process works. First, the publisher produces the book that the author has written. The publisher ships these books (at its own expense) to bookstores or to a distributor (the middle party between the publisher and bookstore). If the books are sent to a distributor, the distributor sells them to bookstores on consignment (usually through a catalog or a sales call) and ships them to the bookstore at the distributor's expense.

When the bookstore sells a book, it pays the distributor or publisher. However, each party in the sales chain takes a percentage of the revenue from the book's sale before the remainder, the royalty, trickles down to the author. Generally, the bookseller will get 40 percent of the sale, the distributor 20 percent, the publisher 30 percent, and the author 10 percent. (As a self-publisher, you would get 40 percent — the sum of the author's and publisher's shares.) If a book sells for $20, the bookseller will get $8, the distributor $4, the publisher $6, and the author $2.

Also keep in mind that booksellers send back returns (books that don't sell) to the publisher at the *publisher's* expense. Authors receive no income from these books.

An advance on royalties may be the only income you ever see from your book. At least it is nonrefundable.

The advance you may or may not receive from a publisher is an advance on royalties, the author's share in the pot. Based on the example above, if you've received an advance of $5,000, that means the publisher needs to sell 2,500 books (2,500 x $2) before it makes back the money it paid in the advance and before you will receive any more royalties. If the publisher doesn't sell enough copies of a book to recoup the advance, then that will be the only money you will ever see. One benefit is that the author doesn't have to pay back the advance if book sales go in the hole.

A bestselling author once told me he was so disappointed in the publishing process that he didn't think he would write another book. It was sad because the fellow is a gifted writer. A lot of people are disappointed from a monetary standpoint because they see the advance check and believe it's only the beginning of more.

The Pros and Cons of Traditional Publishing

Why are authors so eager to hook up with a traditional publisher when there is so little chance of making money? Easy. Books are published on the publisher's dime.

Publishers take care of all the production costs associated with turning a manuscript into a book. They arrange warehousing and distribution. They market the book to bookstores and publicize the book through the media. In return for this service, they pay authors a royalty — a percentage of sales — but their sole purpose in producing books is to make a profit.

In order for publishers to do that, they get authors to sign an exclusive contract, which confirms they are the only publisher that has the right to publish the material for a certain length of time.

When you have signed a contract with a publisher on the basis of a query letter and proposal, you need to deliver the goods. Publishers expect a finished product that is as interesting, marketable, and relevant as your pitch letter asserts it to be. Authors should expect a working, functional, give-and-take relationship with their publisher (and editor). Publishing is a process, and there are many people, from designers to editors to marketing professionals, who work endlessly to support and promote your book. It's ultimately a team effort and everyone on that team needs to recognize the importance of everybody else.

Audrey Bakewell says one misconception many first-time authors have is that publishers are difficult to deal with:

> Mine was always available and easy to work with. I was involved with everything. I had no expenses, which is why I went the traditional publishing route. In comparison, I produced my own video, and the costs will never be recovered.

Design and Layout

There is no doubt you lose some control when you hand over your project to a traditional publisher. The degree of control will depend on the publisher. There should be some give and take on editorial matters. The publisher might like parts of the manuscript and tell the author to redo the rest. At other times the manuscript will be accepted as is with minimal editing.

There is less give and take when it comes to layout and design. Sometimes the publisher will allow input from the author, but more often publishers send a sample of the layout to the author as a courtesy only.

Tom Douglas didn't have much input on his traditionally published books. "They did send me an electronic file of the cover photo they were thinking of using. I've been fairly happy with what they've done with the covers."

Bruce Dowbiggin was only involved with layout and design "if a concept wasn't working. But they always listened."

Jill Lublin recalls:

> I did get a little bit involved in the cover design and layout, mostly just saying, yes, I like it, or I don't like it. It wasn't anything too big. We did have final approval over cover design. We were able to have some input, but I will tell you it was not a great deal. On *Networking Magic*, my second book, we really didn't like the first cover and made them redo it.

According to Stan Fischler:

> Usually, you would like to have as much of a say as possible, but too often they determine the title of the book and the cover of the book. Unless you

have something written in your contract that you have the final say, it's usually the publisher that does.

Publicity and Marketing

Publicity and marketing are generally two separate departments. Publicity refers to book reviews, feature articles, and interviews. The publicist may help you mail out press kits and arrange book signings at larger book chains. Marketing is about advertising and direct mailings.

Decisions made in both departments are all about budgets. The aggressive author who takes the initiative and arranges his or her own promotion and marketing is more apt to squeeze some extra cooperation (and funding) from the publisher. (Note that smaller presses usually have less room to maneuver with their budgets.) If the author waits for the publisher to sell the book, it could hit the remainder table sooner than expected. It is often wise for the author to set aside most or all of the advance money for promotional purposes. Authors who take control of their destiny have a better shot at grabbing the publisher's attention and perhaps receiving an offer to produce a second book.

In fact, when a publisher is choosing which book to publish, the author with a detailed and legitimate marketing and promotional plan rises to the top of the pile. If the author does not take the initiative in driving the sales of a book, it is more likely to fail.

Sometimes, even the best plans of an author are thwarted by a reluctant publisher, as illustrated by this story from Tom Douglas:

> I think the biggest misconception is that traditional publishers are altruistic people who really want to see talented writers succeed. I have a friend who sold a coffe-table book to a large publisher. A bunch of us put our heads together and came up with a promotion where we would have a launch at a press club. One of us even had a lead-in to a well-known family where there was a strong possibility that a member of this family would attend because of their identifying with the book's topic and because we would give part of the proceeds of any books sold at the event to one of their favorite

causes. The publisher wouldn't give us the green light on this. I hear stories like this all the time.

In the United States, many publishers are under the umbrella of a major conglomerate. The subsidiary publishers in each conglomerate might share resources and personnel. Under such circumstances, it is easy for authors to fantasize about the massive media and marketing resources that will ensure their books become bestsellers.

The reality is that publishers don't invest huge resources in marketing every book on their list. Like a fashion buyer who is over in London guessing what the North American public will be wearing six months later, the publisher guesses which 10 books out of 100 will offer the best return for money spent on marketing. Regardless of what a publisher might pay you for an advance, unless your book is one of those top 10, your chances of getting the publisher to pay for even a book tour might be slim. The only way to get around this is to stipulate a promotional budget in your contract.

One final misconception that Tom Douglas addressed was the issue of how exciting it is to see your book in print:

> My wife, Gail, had been a successful author long before me with her 14 romance novels for Bantam. She would tell me that it's the weirdest experience when your first book is accepted. It's almost like the whole process is happening to somebody else or that you're having an out-of-body experience watching the whole thing unfold. I now know what she meant, and even today, when I see my books on the shelf in a Superstore or a Chapters, it's as though I'm looking at something written by someone I know but not really by me. I'm thrilled to see the books there, but it's not the "rush" that I always thought it would be. Perhaps that's because I went through the experience with Gail. We both know it can end on a whim, so we don't take it all too seriously.

5

Vanity, Print-on-Demand, and E-Publishing: Not the Same as Self-Publishing

There are many similarities between vanity publishing, print-on-demand, and e-publishing, but each process has its own unique characteristics. To save yourself thousands of dollars, investigate which one fits your needs. If you decide to go one of these routes, check out the firm before you sign a contract. While there are many legitimate firms available to publish your manuscript, there are also companies more interested in your money than in production quality.

Vanity Publishing

Imagine a publisher that charges an author for all the costs of publishing a book and then sells that same book back to the author for an additional charge. That's what usually happens when an author signs up with a vanity press.

For the publisher, it's the perfect world. There is little financial risk involved. The authors pay for the cost of everything — the publisher's profit and overhead, all layout, printing, and promotion costs — and they generally pay much more than they would if they coordinated the printing themselves. In fact, if you paid a printing company to print copies of your book, the books would be your property. In the case of vanity publishing, the books remain the property of the publisher until you buy them, even though you have paid for the layout and printing. Finally, the publisher offers no editing, warehousing, or distribution. If your book is going to sell, you have to get out and promote it yourself, usually after you have bought dozens or hundreds of copies.

Lyle Manery hasn't had a personal experience with a vanity publisher, but one of his friends did:

> One of my friends went with a vanity press, in spite of my cautions. I reviewed the contract and suggested changes, to which they readily agreed. The kicker was that they convinced my friend of the value of their services, which in my opinion were negligible. One of the implied promises was that they could help her get into *other* markets. The company used arguments such as, "You will be able to sell enough books, from the back of the room, to pay for the printing before the book is printed." Of course that was nonsense. Another implied benefit was having more speaking engagements in the physical location of the vanity press. More nonsense! I wish I could tell you a happy ending and that my warnings were proven wrong. However, it cost over $7.50 per book to have 2,000 books prepared by this vanity press. The total cost of production was over $20,000, and the books did not sell. My estimate is that we could have had this book printed, cover and all, for less than $3.00 per book.

Warren Redman knew a couple of people who were vanity published. "I don't think they sold any books apart from to their family and a few friends."

Tom Douglas has "read all the horror stories about people mortgaging their homes to pay for thousands of copies that end up moldering away in their garage or basement."

Jill Lublin, on the other hand, has a more positive reaction, though with a caveat:

Vanity publishing? Yes, I know quite a few people who have had experience with it. I think it's actually a really good solution for a lot of people. The [two] biggest issues with books … are publicity and distribution. You have to have both of them. It's key. The problem with vanity publishing is they can get your book out, but it's still totally up to you to then do publicity and distribution. If you're going to find a vanity publisher, find one who has some distribution contacts in place.

The problem with vanity publishing is that you pay more than you need to, and then still have to do all the marketing and distribution.

What to Watch Out For

Vanity presses will often advertise for authors in writing magazines and newsletters, though they will deny they are vanity presses. These ads might say "Manuscripts Wanted" or "Authors Wanted." Traditional publishers do not advertise for books and writers. If you see a "Call for Authors," you can be sure you'll need to dust off your checkbook.

Vanity publishers claim to be picky about choosing authors, but they will accept any manuscript as long as the author pays the upfront fee. After you've submitted your manuscript for their consideration, you will usually receive a glowing acceptance letter that tells you how wonderful your book is. The "vanity" designation came about because of the rave reviews these presses bestow on their authors' manuscripts. In reality, conventional booksellers and even libraries will reject these books. One reason is that they are often poorly written or of no general interest (conventional publishers have already rejected many of these manuscripts). Another reason is that the design and layout, things the author will generally have no control over, may also be of poor quality.

A vanity contract can be vague. It doesn't usually itemize how much of the fee is for printing or layout, or how much is for the national promotion the publisher might say it carries out. Authors will pay anywhere from $10,000 to $30,000, depending on size and length, for the privilege of having their books vanity published.

Always go through the contract carefully to search for hidden costs and other surprises. Hidden charges might include a setup fee or deposit, although the company may deny you are paying for the actual publishing. It may even promise to refund the fee, but the company can always come up with a reason not to follow through on the refund. It could tell you the layout was more complicated than expected or there was some other unforeseen problem. If the contract doesn't itemize the exact fees for printing and layout, it's difficult to argue.

Another item to watch out for is a prepurchase requirement. The contract may say you have to purchase a large quantity of books — hundreds or even thousands — or the company may insist you presell a set number of books before they are published.

Instead of paying printing and layout costs, you may have to pay a large sum for editing, although the result would be a substandard, rather than professional, job. You could end up paying for a publicity campaign you didn't anticipate, and if such a campaign increases sales or brings more revenue to the publisher, you're unlikely to realize any benefit in the form of a price reduction.

If a vanity publisher does offer marketing and promotion, chances are it will just list the book on its website or in its e-catalogue. In most cases, fewer than 100 copies are ever sold. For any sales that do occur, vanity publishers might promise the author 40 percent royalties and 80 percent subsidy rights for each book sold. However, they won't make any promises regarding sales. After all, where is the incentive for them to sell the author's book? Because their fees are so inflated, they make their money printing the book. Spending time or money to promote or market the book would only cut into their profits.

When you sign the contract, you've actually signed over the exclusive license for the publisher to exploit your work. The vanity publisher owns the books. You, the author, might receive ten copies for your own use and the opportunity to purchase more books at a discount, but you will have to pay *something* for any additional books, even though you've paid all the costs of producing your own book.

Be aware that some vanity publishers will use misleading terminology to pull in unsuspecting authors. They may describe themselves as joint venture, cooperative, or subsidy presses in their advertising, or use phrases like "shared responsibility" and even "self-publishing." Some try to pass themselves off as conventional or small press publishers. A subsidy, joint venture, or cooperative firm is similar to a vanity publisher. The author pays for printing and binding, although the publisher may subsidize some costs. The subsidy publisher may offer editing, warehousing, distribution, and perhaps even some marketing — for a cost. They may do limited screening of manuscripts to weed out controversial and illegal material, but it's still all about the money. Completed books are still the property of the publisher, and authors will only receive a royalty when books are sold. It's unlikely authors will ever recoup the publishing costs they've forked out. In today's publishing market, there are many similarities between vanity, subsidy, and print-on-demand firms.

As in any industry, there will be unscrupulous firms that operate unethically and even fraudulently. Overcharging is one thing, but some will not live up to their contract: they won't deliver the finished books, they will fail to pay royalties, they will make false promises, they may even produce a book of such poor quality that you'll be embarrassed to show anyone.

Perhaps one of the worst experiences for an author is to trust a firm that takes his or her money and manuscript, and then runs. The author would lose all the time and creativity he or she put into the book. It is also possible for one of these deceitful firms to publish a manuscript different from the one the author provided and pass it off as an edited version.

Do your due diligence, check out any firm before you sign a contract, and beware of excessive promises. If it sounds too good to be true, it usually is.

Benefits

A vanity publisher isn't always a bad thing. Deepak Chopra had his first book published by a vanity press. Traditional publishers turn down a lot of good manuscripts for many reasons, some of them economical, so vanity publishing does offer an alternative. It gives the author something concrete to market, and for novice authors, it's always worth it for them to see their book in print. However, as I'll explain in chapter 7, as well as in the section "Print-on-Demand" below, it's possible to see your book in print for a much lower price than you would pay a vanity publisher.

If You Decide to Go with a Vanity Publisher

Before making the decision to go with a vanity publisher, you may want to check out the company to ensure it will be there next week, after you fork over your money. You may also want to investigate

Beware of any vanity publisher that promises mega-profits.

the quality of its finished product. You can do that by asking to see the publisher's catalog or by purchasing a couple of titles it has already published. Contact some previous clients for a reference. Try to find out if the company keeps its promises.

Know that literary agents and qualified editors don't work with vanity publishers, so if you receive a referral from this type of source, it's highly questionable. Watch out for some of the following other warning signs:

- Promises of mega-profits
- Promises not backed up in a contract
- Vagueness about what it will cost to publish
- Offers to split costs
- Outlandish praise
- Profit or sales guarantees
- Promises that your book will get into bookstores
- Any kind of pressure
- Refusal to answer legitimate questions

Two better-known vanity publishers are Vantage Press and Dorrance Publishing. Both are well established and provide similar services.

Vantage Press, <www.vantagepress.com>, offers a 40 percent royalty fee on the retail price of the book and publishes most manuscripts that are submitted. It will, however, screen for hard-core pornography and books that might be libelous or defamatory. Vantage offers to send out media review copies, to solicit both online and traditional booksellers, and perform other types of promotion.

Dorrance Publishing, <www.dorrancepublishing.com>, has a detailed website that lists testimonials, reviews written about its authors, and several author resources. It offers two basic packages: traditional subsidy publishing and self-publishing/private publishing. The traditional subsidy publishing package includes manuscript editing, layout and design, printing and binding, warehousing and distribution, and invoicing and collections. It also obliges Dorrance to republish books when the initial supply is depleted for no extra cost. The self-publishing/private publishing package also offers manuscript editing, layout and design, and printing and binding, as well as a promotion option. Both packages copyright the book in the author's name.

Ron and Adrianna Edwards sum up this type of publishing by saying:

> Vanity publishing has its upside, but in general it has a very bad reputation. What they do is take your manuscript, lay it out, print it, and bind it for a fee or a unit price. Then X number of books are delivered to you and it is up to you to sell them. With Amazon and other online services, this is easier than ever before, but do your homework. Some of these vanity presses have terrible reputations. Find out what you get and how much it will cost. You can always hire an editor and a designer and print the thing yourself, often for cheaper than the vanity house can do it.

Print-on-Demand

Print-on-demand (POD) companies try to make "self-publishing" affordable. They cut down on the printing costs because books are printed only when an order is placed. Instead, the author pays an upfront processing fee that can range from $99 to $1,500 and up, depending on the service package. This processing fee covers the POD company's costs to design and lay out the book. These companies will sometimes offer marketing, distribution, and fulfillment services as well, for additional costs. Then, when orders come in for the book, the author also pays the cost of printing, which is usually at a high unit cost per book because it's much more expensive, per book, to print small runs than larger runs.

For authors who want to have a few copies of their book on hand, but who don't want the hassle of doing it themselves, print-on-demand is an excellent option. However, the chances of getting these books into bookstores are slim. Booksellers traditionally stock books they can return to the publisher for full credit. That isn't the case with POD. If you have a good promotional campaign and people go into bookstores specifically to ask for your book, the store may process it as a special order, but don't hold your breath.

Lyle Manery believes that POD is a great idea if you are not sure how many books you will sell:

> You can test the market with a short run. Perhaps you only need a small number of books for friends and relatives. If you need more copies later, you can simply order them. However, I have found it is best to have a minimum order of either 50 or 100 books if you want to save money. On any order under 500 books, it may be financially effective to use a print-on-demand printer. Another useful approach with print-on-demand is to guarantee an order of 500 books, to be printed in small batches over a period of two years.

If you can negotiate this, you should be able to get a much cheaper per book rate.

Ron and Adrianna Edwards agree that POD makes a lot of sense in many cases:

> The risk is much less than printing several hundred or thousand copies that sit in a warehouse unsold. The unit costs are quite a bit higher, but the risk is minimal. One caution is editorial. POD companies generally do not edit your book. That is your responsibility. Ditto typesetting and design. These are expensive processes, but do not try to skip them or the book will suffer, as will your credibility.

What to Watch Out For

Some POD companies try to pass themselves off as a self-publishing service. They might even allow authors to set up their own imprints. However, in self-publishing, the author controls the layout, design, and every aspect of the publishing process. With POD, you'll have a choice of two or three design templates and a series of service packages. The overall look of the book is up to the company. Rarely will these firms publish anything but softcover books.

Reputable POD firms will produce a trade paperback within a reasonable time frame. They will offer an attractive royalty on the retail price; produce a full-color cover; allow for inside photos; look after the International Standard Book Number (ISBN), bar code, and Cataloging in Publication (CIP) registration (see chapter 6);

provide an electronic proof and printed proof; offer the option of a Portable Document Format (PDF) e-book; and allow the author to retain all rights.

Unfortunately, POD technology opens the door to unqualified, unprincipled, and deceitful individuals who are basically vanity publishers pretending to be independents. They promise riches and fame but offer no distribution or promotion. Most of the time, they will sell fewer than 100 books. These firms will hide fees, such as prepurchase or preselling obligations, in the contract's small print. They might entice authors by offering a small advance, anywhere from ten to a couple of hundred dollars, but that is just a marketing ploy — they'll get that money back from the author in fees and overpricing.

Less-scrupulous POD firms will use low-quality paper stock and poor production values. They will demand that the author sign over exclusive publishing rights to the company for a period of time. The author might also incur extra charges for things like reprints, cover design, ISBN, bar code, and copyright registration, as well as incurring accessibility fees (to keep the book in distribution). It may be up to the author to ensure the book is listed in Bowker's *Books in Print* and that it has CIP or Library of Congress Control Number (LCCN) data.

When it comes to POD, costs are all over the map — even though most firms use the same printer to produce their books and have minimal overhead. Most only have a storefront office and a website. In spite of this, they will charge more to produce a book than you would pay if you were coordinating your own printing and design. For some POD firms, the name of the game is up-selling services you don't need and marketing that doesn't work, which they will deem is mandatory. These firms end up resembling the shady side of vanity publishing.

Like vanity publishers, POD firms do not pick and choose the manuscripts they publish. If an author is willing to pay the fees, the firm will publish the book. They will, however, offer editing and proofreading services at an extra cost.

Also like vanity publishers, they may claim that your book will be stocked in major bookstores. Even a traditional publisher can't guarantee this, and POD publishers are often held in the same low regard as vanity presses by booksellers and reviewers. Booksellers will balk, as mentioned earlier, at the POD policy of prepaid orders and nonstandard industry discounts. Media generally ignore PODs because there is no editorial filtering. POD publishers may argue that most copies are sold over the Internet, but fewer than 10 percent of books are sold online.

Any marketing or media packages offered by a POD firm are likely not going to make much difference to your sales, but you should at least make sure that your book is listed in the POD's catalog and on its website.

If you manage to interest a royalty publisher in your POD book, there may be issues in your POD contract that affect the subsequent release through conventional publishing. Technically, the POD book never goes out of print, so the rights to publish it may never revert to you. You should make sure your contract is non-exclusive (this means you can place the book with another publisher) or that it includes a clause stating an end date for your agreement with the POD firm and/or a clause that allows you to terminate the contract at an earlier date if you find another publisher or if you have conflicts with the POD firm (over editorial issues, pricing, print quality, royalties, etc.) that can't be resolved. You should be aware, though, that many traditional publishers will not be interested in taking on a book that has been previously published by POD or vanity presses.

Benefits

Most of the time, a POD firm allows the author to keep his or her rights, and the author also receives royalties on books sold.

POD technology allows some older books to stay in print for a longer time than they normally would. Traditional publishers will use a short-run printing firm to resurrect out-of-print books so they don't have to fund a large print run.

PODs also solve the problem of storing large quantities of books. Books are printed, trimmed, and bound as ordered. New technologies allow them to be of equal quality to a traditionally published book. However, they do cost more on a per-book basis.

If You Decide to Go with a Print-on-Demand Publisher

Use the same due diligence as suggested for checking out the legitimacy of a vanity publisher. Contact some of the POD firm's clients to see if it delivered on its promises. Order a couple of POD books to see the quality. Is the company's name listed on any warning lists? (One of the best warning lists is located on the WritersWeekly website, <www.writersweekly.com>.) Try to find out how long the firm has been in business. Does it seem like a stable, legitimate company? Imagine how you would feel if your rights were passed on to a third party without your permission if the firm went bankrupt after receiving your check.

If you decide to publish with a print-on-demand firm, make sure you do your research.

As you would with any other contract, make sure you know what you're getting into. POD contracts are not standardized, so read the fine print. Get a guarantee on per-book costs. Regarding production, ask about the options for, and the quality of, paper, binding, cover, layout, and design. What is the company's time frame for filling orders?

Royalty rates may be misleading; determine if they are based on a net price rather than a retail price. Also watch out for a clause that states some of the terms and conditions can change without warning.

Xlibris and iUniverse are two of the largest fee-based print-on-demand firms. They don't screen manuscripts, and their publication fees range from one end of the scale to the other. Authors receive a royalty on sales.

Xlibris offers three levels of service. With the basic service, authors choose from layout and cover templates to create a trade paperback. The professional service gives a larger choice of templates, and the author can customize them. This package allows for tables and an index, and also has both hardcover and paperback options. The custom service incorporates the same features as the professional package, but authors are allowed to speak directly to the Xlibris designer to further customize their books. The company also produces books in full color.

Xlibris has set up an online bookstore through which the authors can sell their books. According to *Publishers Weekly* (March 17, 2003), since the company's inception in 1997, Xlibris paid out US$1 million in royalties to approximately 9,000 authors, which translates to about US$111 per author. *The Wall Street Journal* (April 24, 2004) reported that Xlibris published 10,269 titles through March 25, 2004, of which 352 sold more than 500 copies and 1,453 sold over 200 copies. The average sale of books per publication is about 130 copies (information taken from <www.parapub.com/statistics>).

iUniverse offers four packages, which all include a specified number of free paperback books, quick availability, one-on-one author support, author discounts, online bookstore listing, trade paperback format, and non-exclusive contracts. Optional services listed are line editing, proofreading, hardcover format, bookselling materials, and co-op advertising.

Booklocker.com charges a minimal setup fee and a small annual POD file-hosting fee. There is a choice of templates for creating an original cover (to which the author retains the rights), again for a reasonable fee, and if authors want to use their own cover art, there is no extra charge.

Trafford Publishing offers six publishing packages and, like Xlibris, includes full-color books. Trafford reports that when it began its publishing operations in 1995, it was the first company to introduce the concept of on-demand publishing for black-and-white trade books.

E-Publishing

E-books are electronic books, most commonly in a PDF format, that can be read on any computer with Adobe Reader. Several POD companies offer the option of an e-book in their package of services. Because there are no physical printing costs involved, many authors think they will get rich going this route. Before you count your millions, look at your own world. Do you buy e-books? Do your friends and family?

In e-publishing, even more than any other type of publishing, it's important to know who your reader is. That's because an e-book exists only on a website. Putting an e-book on a website does nothing to attract readers. You have to have a focused, effective marketing plan to let readers know your book is available.

There are certain kinds of manuscripts that work well as e-books, as Lyle Manery points out:

> At present, I have two e-books. Both started as regular books. *Vital Knowledge for Your Retirement Planning* was written with a specific group of buyers in mind. They purchased 5,000 copies before the book went to press. The second book, *The*

Ultimate Tax Shelter, was published as a short-run book or print-on-demand. Only 500 copies have been printed.

With *Vital Knowledge*, there is some information that changes every year or two, such as amounts paid by the Canada Pension Plan or by Old Age Security. There was no way this book could be updated and republished every year. As an e-book, I can make changes as often as necessary.

The Ultimate Tax Shelter was a natural for the e-book market. Frankly, I got tired of selling it through traditional channels. It is easy to e-publish. To do it well, you should write the book, have it edited and styled, and create an attractive cover. In short, you do everything just as though you are preparing it for a traditional publisher. When it is ready, you can save it to PDF for easy online reading. Then upload it on your website or find someone else to publish it on his or her own website. It's actually good to have both a printed and an e-book version available. So far, I have not sold a large number of e-books. However, I have sold more e-books than printed versions from my websites during the same period of time. In order to make sales from your website, you need to have steady traffic. I am still working on that. Having a good newsletter is a good way to get going.

What to Watch Out For

E-books are usually created in Adobe Acrobat. The purchaser needs compatible reader software such as Adobe Reader to be able to open the file.

When you have your manuscript e-ready, your e-publisher may require the text in MS Word, text only, PDF, or HTML format. Your setup fee may include layout and cover art, or the cover may cost extra. You should have the book professionally edited before you submit it to the publisher.

Apart from the setup fee, you may be required to pay a monthly, quarterly, or annual hosting fee. Author royalties will vary from firm to firm. You do have the right to ask questions about your

If you go with an e-publisher, remember that its website will reflect on your book's professionalism.

e-publisher's accounting records, and you should receive or have easy access to regular sales reports. Ideally, you will have a password so you can access these reports online 24 hours a day.

Any e-publisher that avoids questions about rights, royalties, and sales reports; charges outlandish fees; offers an advance on royalties in exchange for all rights; or doesn't post terms online is suspect. You should run away as fast as you can.

Benefits

The main advantages of e-publishing are that there are no printing costs, no minimum orders, no warehousing, and no postage or courier costs.

You also have the option of hosting the book on your own website. But how do you keep people from freely copying the e-book and e-mailing it to all their friends?

Digital rights management (DRM) is a term for a range of technologies that restrict files from being freely distributed. Files may be encrypted or digitally marked so that only one reader can "unlock" a file. Think of it as a password-protected file that can't be distributed from one computer to another.

If You Decide to Go with an E-Publisher

The same principles apply for e-books as for any type of publishing. Do a background check when soliciting an e-publisher. Look at the catalog, contact some of the authors for references, and see if the company delivers on its promises.

Is the contract an exclusive arrangement? You need to scrutinize the contract to be absolutely clear on the publishing rights you are turning over and if there is a termination and rights reversal clause. What you don't want to do is turn over the rights to all publishing venues. You want the contract to be specific to e-publishing only. Never, never, never give up all your rights.

You want to make sure the publisher has a good reputation. You should steer clear of those that don't accept credit card payments and have poorly designed websites. Their website will reflect on your book's professionalism. Cheesy websites don't give readers much confidence, especially when they're using credit cards.

Booklocker.com and iUniverse are two of the more well-known e-publishers.

Booklocker.com pays 70 percent royalties on the list price of e-books sold through its website. The contract is nonrestrictive (i.e., the publisher doesn't retain exclusive rights to publish), with an easy termination clause. Booklocker asks for non-exclusive rights, which means you can sell and distribute e-books through other venues. It also has a careful screening process for manuscripts and uses creative marketing options to help create sales. Booklocker is linked to the popular *WritersWeekly* newsletter and website.

iUniverse, which was awarded the Editor's Choice award by *PC Magazine,* asks for nonexclusive rights for e-book publishing. Its e-contract is an addendum to the POD publishing packages. Royalties are listed at 50 percent of the net price of the e-book, and authors receive quarterly royalty statements.

AuthorHouse allows authors to retain all the rights to their books and select their own royalty schedule. It provides personal support through the publishing process and offers various levels of service, including prepublishing, publishing, promotional, and bookselling.

6

So You've Decided to Self-Publish

After reading about traditional publishers, vanity presses, print-on-demand, and e-books, you may wonder if you should self-publish your book. There are several reasons authors do, but perhaps the main reason is control.

When you let someone else publish your book, you always give up some level of control, whether it's editorial or layout. If control is everything to you, then you will not regret going the self-publishing route.

The following are some of the other reasons authors might self-publish:

- Traditional publishers rejected the book, and the author is too passionate about the subject not to have it published. Rejection doesn't always mean a manuscript is bad. The publisher may not see the book's commercial potential, or the book may not fit the company's editorial guidelines. Publishers also tend to shy away from books on controversial subjects or niche topics.

- You retain control over marketing. Conventional or traditional publishers don't always get books into bookstores. Except for the odd publisher-sponsored promotional event, it's often up to the author to sell the book anyway. If you

If you self-publish, you can set your own timeline. The process will likely be faster than going with a traditional publisher.

leave sales exclusively to the bookstores or the publisher, chances are the book will end up on the discount table sooner rather than later.

- You can make more money. This may be particularly important if the book is aimed at a small, specific audience. If you know that audience and how to connect with it, it might make sense to self-publish and implement your own targeted marketing plan, collecting 100 percent of net sales proceeds instead of 10 percent. You also have more control over discounting, which is something you can use to entice bulk sales.

- The book ties in with an event, and the timeline makes it impractical to go with a regular publisher. There is no question that going with a traditional publisher can be a painfully slow process. You're working on their schedule, not yours. Rob Lennard, a successful commercial real estate agent in Calgary, Alberta, wrote a children's book that received rave reviews and numerous sales almost overnight. He recounts how he made his decision:

> I didn't want to waste time looking for a publisher. I was on a tight timeline in that I was releasing the book on the Family Day holiday [in February] in front of over 700 people. I had confidence that my book/CD was good enough to receive corporate funding, in exchange for placing a company's logo on the cover. [A company came on board and covered not only the cost of making the CD — included in the book — but also the cost of the first printing.] The only thing I had written prior to my book was a one-page poem ten years prior. However, I discovered no books existed on my subject for Alberta elementary school kids. That said, I wasn't sure if I would create a well-received book or a dud. As it turned out, the book is surpassing my wildest imagination and is well on its way to becoming a Canadian bestseller.

Any type of book can be self-published: fiction, nonfiction, children's, reference, short stories, poetry, even coffee-table books. But don't self-publish a book for the sake of having a book or because you can't find a conventional publisher (see chapter 1).

Self-published authors are in good company, as you can see from the sidebar "Some Famous Self-Published Authors." Even those authors who have previously placed books with traditional publishers may decide to retain their rights and self-publish. This gives them more control over profits and over discounting for special sales and promotions. Self-publishing authors can also bring books to the market much more quickly. Lyle Manery says:

> I never approached a traditional publisher or any other publisher for that matter. *No Salesman Will Call?* was my second book, and I thought I knew how to do it myself. So far, it has sold over 5,000 copies.

Most book buyers don't ask who published a book. They don't collect books based on the publisher. The average buyer assumes that if a book is in the bookstore, a conventional publisher published it.

Steps to Self-Publishing

Perhaps you sent your manuscript out to agents and publishers and didn't receive a bite. Or maybe you decided right at the start to publish the book yourself and retain control over the process. In either case, there are several steps you need to take before your book is ready to hit the bookstore shelves:

- Find a designer
- Design the cover
- Design and typeset the text
- Proofread the laid-out text
- Obtain ISBN, CIP/LCCN, and bar code information
- Request printers' quotes (see chapter 7)
- Set a price

You may end up doing several of these steps at the same time or finding yourself going back to fine-tune an earlier decision.

Some Famous Self-Published Authors

There is no shame in self-publishing and no shortage of self-published authors in the marketplace. Some you may have heard of: Virginia Woolf (who, with her husband, ran a publishing house that produced books by other authors as well as her own), Rudyard Kipling, D.H. Lawrence, and Zane Grey, to name a few.

- Mark Twain self-published *The Adventures of Huckleberry Finn* because he had issues with his previous publishers. The proceeds from the book helped him fund the development of one of the first working typewriters.

- Leo Tolstoy paid 4,500 rubles to publish his first novel, *War and Peace.*

- Edgar Allen Poe self-published some of his work.

- Tom Peters self-published *In Search of Excellence* and sold more than 25,000 copies in the first year. After that, he sold the rights to a conventional publisher.

- With his friends' help, James Joyce paid for the 1922 printing of *Ulysses.*

- Howard Fast's involvement in the Communist Party kept publishers at bay, so he published *Spartacus* himself in 1951.

- *The Tale of Peter Rabbit* was self-published by author Beatrix Potter after a publisher initially rejected it, afraid of the illustration costs. The publisher then changed its mind in 1902 after seeing the self-published version and thought about the commercial possibilities. The book has subsequently sold over 40 million copies and was translated into 35 languages.

- Irma Rombauer used $3,000 of her own money to publish *The Joy of Cooking* in 1931.

- George Bernard Shaw self-published some of his writings before he became famous.

- Nathaniel Hawthorne, who wrote *The House of the Seven Gables* and *The Scarlet Letter,* self-published his first book.

- Ernest Hemingway and T.S. Eliot self-published their first books.

- James Redfield sold 80,000 copies of *The Celestine Prophecy* from the trunk of his car before it sold to a conventional publisher.

- Walt Whitman self-published some of his poems.

- Deepak Chopra vanity-published his first book before selling the rights to a traditional publisher, where it became one of his bestsellers.

- Benjamin Franklin used the pen name Richard Saunders to self-publish *Poor Richard's Almanack* in 1732.

- Dave Chilton self-published *The Wealthy Barber.*

- Richard Nixon self-published *Real Peace.*

- Ken Blanchard and Spencer Johnson initially self-published *The One Minute Manager.* Experts told them they would never sell such a short book for $15. It took them three months to sell over 20,000 copies in San Diego alone.

Working with Designers

Unless you already are one by trade, hire a professional designer to design and typeset your book. Know what you want up front and consider your reader. For example, if most of your readers will be elderly, you'll want to use a larger type size than you would in a book aimed at young people. Every designer will have a different idea about what he or she thinks is appropriate. A good one will be able to advise you, but you may also find you have to lead your designer in the direction you want to go, while allowing his or her creativity to embellish the end result.

Your first priority in choosing a designer is to see if he or she can meet your needs. Has the designer worked on a book project? If not, does he or she have the tools and knowledge to start? (Note that many of the same methods are used in preparing annual reports.) Can the designer prepare the finished product in a format printers will accept? Look at the designer's portfolio. Can he or she produce the look you want to achieve? Is the designer sensitive to your budget? Can he or she meet your deadline?

You will save a lot of time and money by having a vision of how you want your book to look. Check out other book covers (front and back) and layouts. You might have three or four examples of each. Maybe sketch out a rough layout and share the outline of what your book is about. That, with the samples you provide, will help the designer come up with something close to your idea in the first attempt. Otherwise, the designer is guessing, and you both end up frustrated because nothing he or she prepares comes close to your vision. Communicate. It will cut down on expenses and aggravation.

Inside the Book

Microsoft Word should not be used to lay out a book. You can use it to write and edit your text, but the manuscript will need to be transferred into a layout program. The best applications to use are QuarkXPress (version 4 or higher), Adobe PageMaker (6.5 or higher), and Adobe InDesign (2 or higher).

The industry standard for book layout is QuarkXPress because it is one of the most stable programs available. It's rare for QuarkXPress to cause changes in a document (e.g., missing text; incorrect characters, such as a box instead of a quotation mark; or changes in the flow of text from page to page) once it gets into the printer's system. This kind of file corruption generally occurs only when the designer or printer has used incorrect fonts (i.e., fonts that were either incompatible or not provided to the printer by the designer) or if there is a version error (i.e., using the wrong version of a program to submit the files to the printer — for example, using an older version of QuarkXPress instead of QuarkXPress 4 or higher).

Many printers now prefer to receive book files as high-resolution PDF files. PDF stands for Portable Document Format, which is a file format created by Adobe Systems as a way to share documents across various platforms. A PDF document retains its appearance (including page breaks, graphics, and color) no matter what computer is used.

A PDF file can be created to various resolution specifications. For example, a photography book will have huge files, but if converted into PDF files, it can be made small enough to e-mail. In order to do that, you have to sacrifice image quality. This isn't the type of PDF file your printer wants. It's best to have your designer talk to the printer to determine the PDF specification requirements.

Your electronic files are usually kept on file with the printer, even though they belong to the publisher (you). If you need to print more books, you simply go back to the printer and order them, without reformatting a single file. The reprints will be done with the most recent files, so if there are any changes to be made in subsequent editions, you must advise the printer.

Covers That Jump Off the Shelf

The cliché is true: people do judge a book by its cover. It's your advertising piece, your marketing tool. It makes the reader determine whether or not your book will appeal to them, whether it's interesting enough to even pick up off the shelf. If you've been in a bookstore lately, you'll see how many books are in competition with yours. That's why the cover is so important.

According to R.R. Bowker, which collects statistics on American book publishing, 175,000 new titles and editions entered the US marketplace in 2003. Divide that by 365 and that's 479 titles per day, which means it is easy for a book to be forever lost on a shelf or inside a catalog.

Para Publishing, <www.parapub.com>, reports that a bookstore browser will spend 8 seconds looking at the front cover and 15 seconds on the back — if they choose to pick up the book. When a sales representative shows the cover to a potential bookseller, he or she looks at the cover and listens to the pitch for an average of about 14 seconds.

Next time you visit a bookstore, pay close attention to covers. Stand about ten feet away and take note of which book covers jump off the shelf. In some ways, the cover is more important to the sale of a book than its contents.

A cover is designed separately from the layout of your text. You may even use a different designer to create it, someone who has experience in graphic design and knows how to use text and graphics to grab people's attention.

In chapter 2 I talked about coming up with a catchy title. Regardless of how catchy it is, it should be set in a font that stands out. Flowery fonts, where you can't tell a "g" from a "j," are too difficult to read. If readers have to work at reading the title, they will pass over the book. Think about how quickly your eye scans a bookshelf. That's how much time you have to get someone's attention.

A sales rep has, on average, 14 seconds to pitch a book to a bookseller.

Too much text will also push your book to the bottom of the pile. As in advertising, use the KISS formula, "Keep It Simple, Simon." Putting the whole 200 pages of your book on the front cover will not get people interested. On the other hand, your front-cover text should reflect the contents of the book. Don't waste the reader's time by making him or her guess.

Always test your cover design by stepping back a few yards to see how it might look from across the aisle. Ideally, you want a book cover that will capture someone's attention before he or she even reaches the book's spot on the shelf.

Don't forget to proofread the cover. Several years ago, an organization I worked for ordered 30,000 full-color brochures for a conference. About ten people took turns proofreading the text. When all the boxes of brochures arrived from the printer, we opened the first one and *bam!* An error jumped off the cover fold. A big error in the name of the conference. It was too late. We had signed off on the proofs before going to press, so we couldn't blame it on the printer, and it was not cost-effective to reprint 30,000 brochures a week before the event.

While your front cover should be simple and straight to the point about what the book is about, the back cover can describe the contents in more detail, but not too much detail — just enough to make people buy the book. It is also a good idea to include a blurb about the author that indicates what makes you qualified to write the book.

Again, make sure the fonts are legible. No flowery stuff. Use something like Arial, Times Roman, Verdana, Tahoma, or other straightforward fonts that don't make you guess what the letters are.

If you can't trust your own judgment, get your designer to print off a copy of the cover design so you can show it to several people to get their opinion. Would this be something they would be embarrassed to have on their shelf? If it is, you may need to go back to the drawing board, literally! A lousy cover means fewer sales.

If your budget allows for it, it can be a good idea to have the designer prepare two or three rough covers with different approaches and ask several people which one they like best.

Photographs and Other Images

Will your cover have a picture? If so, keep in mind that pictures, like words, are copyrighted material. You should obtain a release from the photographer before using a photographic image (you can use a version of the permission request letter in Sample 1). Photographers will also want to be paid for use of that image. Even images downloaded from the Internet have copyrights attached.

Your front cover is a marketing piece. Bookstore and publishing catalogs, media publicity, flyers, bookmarks — everything that promotes your book will show the front cover. You need to make sure nobody will come running back to you after the fact and ask you — or sue you — for the perceived riches they think you've made off the book and his or her photograph. Be careful with images.

If you are the photographer and your subject is a person, you may still need a signed release, especially if that person is a celebrity. Some celebrities will want to be paid for use of their photo on the cover. You may use a consent form similar to the one shown in Sample 5 to obtain permission for a person's name or image to be used in your book.

If running around to get a signed release doesn't appeal to you or is logistically impossible, then check out Getty Images, <www.gettyimages.com>, to look for images you can purchase with the release already built in.

To prevent blurred imagery, cover photographs must be high resolution (300 to 600 dots per inch or DPI). Keep that in mind if you decide to purchase online images. While it will cost you a bit more for a higher resolution image, the quality of the photograph determines the quality of your cover. Remember this if you ever think about using the ugly clip art that comes with your computer word-processing system.

If you are using photographs on the back cover or inside the book, you might only need to credit the photographer. However, some photographers will still ask to be paid. If the photos are from a company archive, or if it's a history book, crediting the photo source may be all that's required. Any time you're in doubt about the use of a photograph, contact a publishing lawyer for advice.

SAMPLE 5
SAMPLE RELEASE/CONSENT FORM

Name_____

Project/Written Title_____

Participation_____

Date_____

Location_____

I have participated on the project as indicated above. I hereby grant permission to use my name/image in connection with this project.

I agree that my participation in this project may be deleted at your sole discretion. I consent to the use of my name, likeness, voice, and biographical material in connection with this project publicity and related promotional purposes. I expressly release to you, your agents, employees, licensees, and assigns from and against any and all claims that I have for invasion of privacy, defamation, copyright, or any other cause of action arising out of the production, distribution, publication, or exhibition of the project.

Signature_____

Address_____

_____

Date_____

There Is No Such Thing as Too Much Editing

You can never spend too much time editing. Remember the seven-times rule described in chapter 3? There, it referred to editing your manuscript before it was laid out. Once the designer has formatted the book, you need to check it again. A lot can happen between your PC and the designer's computer. This is especially true when files are going from PC to Macintosh or vice versa. Text might disappear or get garbled, and chapters might get out of order.

These are some things to look out for once your book has been laid out in pages:

- Look for sentences where the words are spaced too loosely or too tightly. The designer should be able to fix this.

- Watch for bad hyphenation. It looks better if there are no more than two line-ending hyphens in a row, and you want to avoid having a hyphenated word at the bottom of a page. Also, watch for bad word breaks, like a proper name that is broken over a line or words like "reap-pear" and "read-just."

- Check for consistency in fonts, chapter headings, subheadings, and spacing between headings and text or captions and photos.

- Check for extra spaces after periods. You should have one space at the end of sentences, so in the typeset file, watch for places where you omitted the space or where you put in two.

- Watch for widows (a short line at the top of a page) and orphans (a single word or part of a word at the end of a paragraph).

- Look for problems with paragraph and line ends. For example, watch for paragraphs that have run together or for lines that end halfway through a sentence, then continue on the next line.

- Don't forget to proofread the photo captions, and make sure the photos are in the right place.

- Make sure the page numbers are in the right order!

Proofreading at the blueline stage is the last chance to catch errors, but making corrections will cost.

After proofreading the layout pages, sit down with the designer and go through the changes page by page. There won't be too many if you did a good job editing before this stage.

The designer will make the corrections, possibly adjust some of the fonts and headings, and send you a final copy. Before he or she sends the electronic files to the printer, you need to go over it one more time to make sure nothing has been corrupted. Keep in mind that most designers are not writers, so they will not catch spelling or grammar mistakes. This is also the point at which you would prepare an index if your book is nonfiction and needs one. If you simply need to index the names of people who figure in your book, you might do it yourself. Otherwise, you can contact the American Society of Indexers, <www.asindexing.org>, or the Indexing and Abstracting Society of Canada, <www.indexingsociety.ca>, to hire a professional indexer. (*The Chicago Manual of Style* has a very useful chapter on indexing.)

Guess what. You're still not done with it yet! The printer will send you the digital blueline. You get to proofread your manuscript one last time. Whatever is on the page at this stage is set in stone. Unless you advise the printer of any errors, the digital blueline is what the finished book will look like. You can't go back and change it after the fact. The printer will usually charge you for changes you make to the blueline, so the more work you do to perfect your manuscript prior to the blueline stage, the less it will cost you.

Professional Touches: ISBNs, CIP Data, and Bar Codes

The International Standard Book Number (ISBN) should be on each and every book published. This number is your book's DNA. It identifies titles or editions of specific publishers. Each number is unique. An ISBN number can never be reused once it's assigned.

Preceded by the letters ISBN, the number is divided into the following four parts:

- Group identifier (for a country, area, or language group; for example, group number 3 is the German language group and group number 982 is the South Pacific region)

- Publisher identifier

- Title identifier

- Check digit (a single end digit, which validates the ISBN. You'll notice some ISBN check digits appear as an uppercase X. This is the Roman number ten.)

Coordinated by the International ISBN Agency in Berlin, group agencies assign ISBN numbers worldwide. R.R. Bowker is the independent agent in the United States, <www.isbn.org>, while Library and Archives Canada, <www.collectionscanada.ca/isbn>, is the agent in Canada.

You must pay for an ISBN in the United States. The fee is determined by how many ISBNs you preorder and will also vary depending on how quickly you need the number.

Application for an ISBN is free in Canada and can be done by completing the online application form on the website listed above.

If you are a Canadian resident, you do not have to apply for an American ISBN, and vice versa. You must apply in the country in which you reside.

According to the ISBN suppliers, the influx of publishers to the marketplace has exhausted the existing numbering system. The system is under revision to increase its numbering capacities. A notice has been sent to publishers that the 10-digit ISBN will change to 13 digits as of January 1, 2007. At that time, all books and book-related products are to have a 13-digit ISBN, and a 3-digit "978" prefix will be affixed to any 10-digit ISBN products in circulation. This affects publishers worldwide. You can obtain more information about ISBNs and the new 13-digit system from <www.isbn-international.org/en/revision.html>, <www.isbn.org>, and <www.bowkerlink.com>.

You will need an ISBN number in order to create a bar code, also known as an EAN code, which is used for retail product marketing. This is similar to a UPC code (Universal Product Code) and is a fixed number of digits. Without a bar code, it's virtually impossible to sell your book through any retail or bookselling outlet. Why limit your marketing possibilities? Make sure that the printer you choose to produce your book is able to create and/or print a proper bar code. Many printers that don't specialize in book printing will not or cannot do this.

You will also need an ISBN number in order to apply for a Cataloging in Publication record (also known as CIP data) in the United States or Canada. The Cataloging in Publication record includes the library cataloging number, which essentially indicates where a book should be shelved in libraries. When you apply for CIP data, you are asked to supply a brief description of the book, a table of contents, the copyright page, a sample chapter, and a copy of the book cover to help determine what the book is about and how it should be cataloged. The CIP record is printed on the copyright page at the front of your book. (See the example on the copyright page of this book.)

There are a couple of benefits to applying for CIP data. For one thing, it makes your book more appealing and credible to librarians. Because the record includes the information a librarian needs to process and shelve your book, a librarian who is thinking of buying your book won't have to do extra work to process it. The national libraries — the Library of Congress in the US and Library and Archives Canada — also use CIP records to compile lists of forthcoming books organized by subject matter. This information is distributed to booksellers and libraries, enabling them to place advance orders. As a result, if your book has been issued a CIP record, you might receive an unsolicited order from a library.

However, applying for a CIP record doesn't necessarily guarantee your book will be assigned one. Self-published books are said to be excluded in both the US and Canada, although exactly how self-published books are identified is unclear.

In the US, the Library of Congress has a two-step process for issuing CIP data. Step one is to be accepted into the program as a publisher. To qualify, a publisher must publish at least three books a year. Therefore the first three books produced by a publisher will likely have to be published without CIP data.

In Canada, the process is less rigorous, but Library and Archives Canada does screen out books produced by large print-on-demand firms that process hundreds of books without any editorial screening (the theory being that many self-published books won't be of interest to librarians). Other books are screened on an individual basis. If your book does not look like a self-published book — meaning it has been professionally edited and designed — its chances of being issued CIP data improve. However, even for traditional publishers, not every book will be assigned CIP data. Due to budget cuts, since 2003, primary and secondary school textbooks are excluded in Canada. If you are denied a CIP record, it is still worth sending two copies of your book for legal deposit with

Library and Archives Canada. Sometimes, if the book is deemed to be of interest to libraries, a CIP record is issued after the fact, and can be used in reprinting.

In summary, a CIP record is useful to have for potential library sales, but you can still market your book through many other channels without it.

Set a Price

A publisher takes many factors into account when determining a book's price. In particular, you need to know what your production costs will be (i.e., editing, design, and printing). Printing costs play a key role and are affected by the following variables:

- The length of your book

- The weight and quality of paper you are using — better paper obviously costs more than cheaper paper

- Whether you plan to include photos; if you are, how many are there and will they be in color?

- The book's format — if the book is an unusual size or shape, it will cost more than a book that is a standard size and shape

- Whether the book is hardcover or softcover (and what type of cover stock you plan to use in either case)

- The number of copies you are going to print

These factors alone will greatly affect the price of your book, and they don't take into consideration the cost of writing, editing, designing, marketing, promoting, and distributing your book.

If you are trying to generate some cash flow by preselling the book, you may need to set a price before you know what your production costs will be. It is common to have a lower prepress price as an incentive for buyers to order ahead of publication, but you don't want to set it too low. You should be able to estimate a reasonable price, comparable to similar books already on the market.

Ideally, whether you are setting a prepress or after-press price, you want to try and make back your production costs, but you must consider the maximum a reader might pay for the book. Sometimes, if the information is specialized and hard to find, you might be able to charge more for your book. It still has to fall within the realm of what everyone else is charging, though. Look at what similar books are garnering at the bookstore. If your book is a softcover, 5" x 7", and 200 pages, it's unlikely anyone will pay $60 for it. Be reasonable. What would you pay for the same book?

You also have to keep in mind the value the reader will get from the book. If your book costs $5 more than your competitor's book, what is it readers will get out of your book that they won't get from others?

According to Lyle Manery,

> Pricing books can be tricky. You want to be able to sell enough to at least cover your costs — not counting the author's time. If you price the book too low, you need to make more sales to break even. If you price the book too high, no one will buy it. What are comparable books selling for? Check it out. As a general rule of thumb you should price your book about five to six times the basic costs of getting the book ready to market. You should include things like editing and design work, cost of the cover, and so on. Assuming you can get it all done for $4 a book, you should charge about $21.95. Remember, after the book is published, there are still marketing and promotional costs. I always calculate a break-even point. Naturally, like everyone else, I would like to make a profit, enough at least to compensate me for my time as an author. As a businessman, nevertheless, my first concern is the return of my financial investment.

Warren Redman uses a similar process, taking into consideration the cost per copy to print and the market prices for similar books. Rob Lennard also looked at what other publishers were charging for similar books.

You may end up experimenting with pricing too. As mentioned above, you can set different prepress and after-press prices for a book. If you've published other books, you can package two or more books together and sell them for less than they would cost separately. You can also raise or lower the price after your book has been available for a while. Just beware that when a book is selling well, raising prices may result in sales coming to a standstill.

7

Working with a Printer to Create a Professional-Looking Book

"When I published my first book, *Eclectic Mushrooms*," says Lyle Manery, "I had very little knowledge about printing and marketing."

> I found a regular printer who claimed he knew something about printing books. However, he did not advise me properly about putting a finish on the cover so the colors would not run together. I printed only 750 copies, fortunately. The last 75 books were basically ruined for lack of a simple varnish coat. The printer blamed me for not advising him to do this. However, I did not understand the process. I relied on his expertise, so how could I advise him?

This is a cautionary tale for potential self-publishers. Many printing firms may say they publish books, but finding a genuine book printer is well worth the extra legwork. It is in your best interest to work with a company that only prints books or at least specializes in book printing. Its employees will know what they're doing, which means it will cost you less to go to them than to other, less specialized printers.

When it comes to printing, local often doesn't mean cheaper.

Some printing firms that are dedicated to books may prefer to work with certain types of books, such as softcover or hardcover, text-only, or art and photography publications. Go to a firm that does the kind of book you are publishing. It will be able to do the job more efficiently and cheaply. A first-time author hired me to edit and project-manage his book. When I was gathering printing quotes, I decided to check out a printer I hadn't tried before. The tried-and-true printer came in at roughly $5,000 for 1,000 copies of a 376-page, 9" x 6" softcover book, while this "new" printer offered to do it for $20,000.

Choose a printer that can meet all your needs. Will it insert the bar code? Will it provide a digital blueline of the text and a digital Kodak proof or color key of the cover? If your distributor has packaging restrictions, can the printer accommodate them? Also make sure your printer does everything under one roof. It usually costs you more if the printer farms out the binding process, for example, or has the cover printed somewhere else.

Don't limit yourself to local printing firms. Local doesn't mean cheaper. Some of the best quotes come from big book-printing companies in other states or provinces, and with the help of e-mail, couriers, and phones, it's not necessary to visit the plant in person. Regardless of where a quote comes from, it can include delivery costs.

The Printing Process: Offset versus Digital

There are two methods of printing books: digital and offset. Many printers will offer one or the other, and you may end up choosing a printer based on the system it uses. For example, if you're not printing a lot of copies of your book, it makes sense to go with a digital printer. For quantities of 1,000 books or more, don't even think about going digital. Offset is much more economical. Some printers may offer both methods, but always ask what process they are using for your book. It makes a huge difference in cost.

Offset Printing

Traditional offset printing involves several stages, including the following:

- Converting book pages into film

- Creating a color composition or blueline for you to proof

- Burning the film onto printing plates

- Running huge sheets through the printing press and pressing the inked plates onto them to print the book

- Allowing the ink to dry

- Folding the big printed sheet into "signatures" (see below)

For example, when printing a 192-page, 6" x 9" book, there would be 12 plates prepared before they reach the press, and 6 signatures to fold afterwards. What's changed in today's process, with publishers submitting manuscripts in computer files rather than on paper, is the ability to go directly to an imaging device that eliminates the need for film.

As mentioned in the previous paragraph, offset pages are printed in groups called "signatures." These collections of pages are printed on one huge sheet that is then folded and bound into the spine of a book along with all the other signatures. If you look closely at some of the books on your shelves, you'll be able to see these page groupings and count how many pages are in a signature. This is why, when some of those old glued bindings get old and cracked, a group of pages falls out of the book rather than just one page. For 32-page signatures there would be 16 pages on each side of a sheet. A 16-page signature would have 8 pages on either side. If the book is a large or unusual size, there may be fewer pages in a signature.

Knowing the size of the signature a printer can produce is important. If you are printing on an offset press, you are always going to have to aim for a certain multiple of pages. It is the most efficient and economical option. Ending up with any number of pages outside the signature complicates the binding process and will cost you more money.

Ask your printer by what increments your pages can increase. This helps you determine your page count when the book is being laid out. For example, for two of my books, the printer told me my page count could go up in increments of eight. After layout, if there were 147 pages, I would either have to take out three pages to make the count 144 or add another five pages to make it 152. You'll notice some books have two or three blank pages at the back. This is to make up the signature rather than cut pages.

Because of the time and money invested in setup, once you get that offset press running, you'd better keep it going. It doesn't make a lot of sense to print fewer than 1,000 books on an offset press. In fact, I recently solicited an offset printing quote for quantities of 1,000 and 500 books. The price was exactly the same.

Digital Printing

A thousand copies is also the number where offset meets digital in price. Small jobs can be done quickly and more cost effectively on a digital press. For this reason, digital printing is particularly popular with print-on-demand companies.

The equipment used in the digital process is similar to a laser printer. You could picture a digital press as a group of large laser printers sitting around waiting for someone to issue the command to print. Of course, it isn't quite that simple, but this is essentially the difference between offset and digital. Once you have the electronic layout, you're ready to go, eliminating all the upfront costs and setup time.

Offset printers press ink onto the page, while digital printers lay toner on the page. Only an expert can tell the difference in terms of text printing. To the naked eye, the text of a digitally printed book will be just as sharp as that produced on an offset press. Where you may see a difference is in picture quality.

For digital printing, signatures are not an issue. Any number of pages is okay for the printing and binding process. Pages are fed into the digital press individually. They are generally trimmed on all four sides, which means they are stuck into the glue binding individually rather than in a signature.

Some printers base the decision to use digital or offset printing on the number of pages in a book and the size of the print run. With longer runs (over 1,000), digital printing is not your best option, at least economically. At that quantity, it is much more cost-effective to go to an offset press. Technology is changing rapidly and dramatically, though, so it may be only a matter of time before the differences are negligible.

Soliciting Printer Quotes

To get an accurate quote for the cost of printing your book, supply the printer with the following information:

- *Your book's title* (to identify the job)

- *Quantity* (the number of copies you want printed). Usually you will ask for quotes on several quantities, perhaps 50, 100, 250, and 500 for digital; 1,000, 2,000, and 3,000 for offset)

- *Page size.* Common sizes (in inches) are 4 x 7; 5¼ x 8¼; 5½ x 8½; 6 x 9; 7 x 9 — and printers may have slight variations on these sizes. If you use a nonstandard size, you'll pay more because the signatures won't fit neatly on one large sheet, and you'll waste a lot of paper when the sheets are trimmed and folded.

- *Number of pages* (in layout form)

- *Paper stock* for both the cover and text

- *Ink color.* Will it be text in black ink only or do you want more colors?

- *Format of the cover.* Will it be full color? Is there any printing on the inside of the cover?

- *Preparation.* What format will you use to submit the files — PDF, QuarkXPress, or other?

- *Type of binding required*

- *Photos.* Will there be photos? If so, how many, and how will they be included in the book — on text pages or in a special photo section? Will they be black and white or in color? Be aware that these decisions will have an impact on the cost of paper stock.

When soliciting quotes from a number of printers, use the same specifications each time so you can get an accurate comparison. Sample 6 is an example of the letter I would send to a number of printers when I was ready to consider printing quotes.

A Note on Paper Stocks

Several paper manufacturing companies produce a wide variety of stocks, in both gloss and matte finishes, that differ in texture and thickness. Cover stocks will be much thicker than text pages. Coated or uncoated text stock can range from 35 to 70 pounds. Your best bet is to ask to look at a sample book.

SAMPLE LETTER REQUESTING PRINTER QUOTES

September 1, 20--

Customer Service
Friendly Printing Co.
1234 Main Street
My Town, MI 56789

Dear Sir or Madam:

I am in the process of publishing a book, *Self-Publishing for Everyone*. The manuscript will be completed for mid- to end July and it needs to be available for distribution in September. I would like to get a quote, based on the following details:

- Quantity: at least 1,000 for first printing (plus costs for subsequent printing)
- Page size: 5.25 x 8.25, no bleeds, bound along 8.25 side
- Pages: 192 to 200 pages plus paperbound cover
- Stock: Text – 60 lb offset – black throughout
- Cover: 10 pt C1S cover; 4-process color plus ½ mil gloss plastic lamination outside only
- Preparation: QuarkXPress for both text and cover with high-resolution images to include all screen and printer fonts
- Binding: Perfect bind, trim and pack in cartons
- F.O.B. Chicago

I trust your quote will include a blueline proof.

There is no printing on the inside cover.

Thanks,

Debbie Elicksen

The cheapest stocks a printer offers are the most popular ones; they're cheap because the printer orders them in large quantities. Every printing firm carries different paper stocks. You should check with different printers to see what they have readily available at their plants. Depending on the size and complexity of a job, they can order in special paper, but you can save a lot of money by sticking to their regular in-house stock.

I can't stress enough that you choose a printer familiar with book publishing.

A Note on Binding

One of the components that factors into the overall cost of a book is binding. When pages are sewn into the binding, it is called saddle stitching. This method is more common with hardcover books. Glued bindings, also called perfect-bound, are more economical than saddle stitching and are preferable for softcover books.

You'll also see some books, such as appointment books and reference guides, that are coil-bound. Coils can be plastic or wire. Printers usually offer a wide choice of colors and coil thickness. A Cerlox binding is similar to coil, but is always plastic and has a plastic strip that forms a spine on which you can print the book's title. It's the least expensive form of binding. Both coil and Cerlox bindings take up more room on a shelf.

When and How to Ask for Quotes

You can see that it's better to solicit quotes when your book is near completion and you have an idea of its length and design — otherwise you'll have to do it twice. You can ask for a preliminary quote to establish your budget, but be aware the figures will change once you have finalized your layout, cover, and other details.

Feel free to solicit as many quotes from as many different printers as you desire. However, I can't stress enough that you choose a printer familiar with book publishing. If you're unsure how much experience a company has, call and ask.

Don't Be Afraid to Ask Questions

Never assume the printer will know what you want the book to look like. Tell them exactly what you expect, right down to the bar code. If you're not sure exactly what you want, don't be afraid to ask.

For example, you may not be sure what type of cover you want, or what kind of text paper you want to use. You can take samples of books you like to a printer and ask him or her to match the paper stock or cover material. Alternatively, most printers have paper and cover samples you can examine for thickness and quality. They should also be able to tell you what the trade-off is between cost and quality. Newsprint may be the cheapest type of paper to use, but it will make your book look cheap as well. There are many inexpensive paper stocks that cost a bit more than newsprint but will make your book look professional. A printer should also be able to advise you on cover treatment (as mentioned in Lyle Manery's anecdote).

If you start talking to printers before you hire a designer, find out from them what format they prefer for receiving book files. If the printer prefers Macintosh formats, you will want to hire a designer who uses a Mac rather than an IBM-compatible personal computer (PC). If you have to convert files from Mac to PC, you may end up incurring extra costs to fix corrupted files. The less the printer has to do to prepare the files for printing, the less expensive the process will be. (Note that although some printers offer to provide graphic design work, you will save a ton of money by hiring your own designer.)

If you already have a designer, you will want to ensure that the printer you choose can receive files in the format he or she is using. Both Mac and PC files can be submitted as high-resolution PDF files, which all printers can easily print from.

Comparing Quotes and Choosing the One for You

Keep in mind that the more copies you print, the cheaper it's going to be per book. However, don't make the mistake of deciding how many books to print based on the unit cost. You may be able to get a unit cost of $0.95 per book if you print 10,000 copies, but are you going to be able to sell that many? This is why you hear about so many authors with mountains of boxes of unsold books in their basements. The more books you need printed, the cheaper the per-book cost will be. Table 1 shows a grid I used to estimate the unit costs of different print runs for a book.

TABLE 1
ESTIMATING UNIT COSTS PER BOOK

Size of print run	10,000	5,000	2,000	1,000
Printing estimate	$12,200	$7,750	$5,080	$4,170
Layout estimate	$3,000	$3,000	$3,000	$3,000
Estimated cost per book	$1.52	$2.15	$4.04	$7.17

Timing Is Everything

Deadlines. You must know the absolute drop-dead deadline by which the printer needs the electronic files, and you must make sure you meet it. Big jobs, like books, are slotted in amongst other jobs. An unreasonable delay can result in your project being bumped and the one after yours moved ahead. That means your job will fall to the back of the line.

When you know the printer's absolute deadline, work your timeline back from that date and give yourself at least a week's cushion before the files are due. For example, if the printer says it needs the files no later than January 30, make January 23 your absolute deadline to deliver the files. Allow yourself time prior to that deadline for editing, layout, proofreading, and corrections.

Let the printer know if there are any special instructions regarding delivery *before* the truck leaves the plant.

Interview with a Printer

Friesens Corporation is one of Canada's biggest book printers. It has a long history of helping community organizations produce local histories, and this has expanded into a booming self-publishing market. Burton Colter was a customer service representative at Friesens when I talked to him in early 2005. He described many of the common problems that come up when Friesens receives jobs from first-time publishers. He emphasized how important it is to communicate with your printer. Colter left Friesens in June 2005 when he moved to a new city.

Preparing Your File for Printing — Fonts and Files

The two most common issues printers encounter are fonts and images. Fonts must be properly supplied with the files — we can't move a job forward without the fonts. There are a whole bunch of licensing issues, so we can't provide the fonts for the customer. Without the fonts, the whole job will stop.

Fonts are a licensed product. In order for a designer to use a font in a book, they actually have to purchase the rights to use that font. Companies like Adobe have huge font libraries that are available and are purchased by the designer so they have a wide spectrum of fonts they can use legally.

When we bring a job in, we run it through a process called preflight. Fonts are one of the primary checks we do to make sure they are in place — supplied with the files, embedded in the files, or otherwise. We also test for image quality resolution and things like bleeds. We do a whole battery of tests on the files to make sure we can run them trouble-free. Far more often with self-publishers, we see a font problem and [problems with] image resolution quality from not having the proper scanning done or not understanding how image resolution works. People think you can download an image from a website and scale it up. They don't realize there is a resolution drop as you increase the size of a scanned image.

We cannot and will not use Word files. It creates nothing but problems for us. Right off the top with a self-publisher, normally they don't have the appropriate desktop publishing application. We do have a process where someone can take a Word file and we provide them with a PDF driver and walk them through the process. It's a fairly new process and a little bit of a challenge getting it up and running for customers. There's a lot of technical support involved. It's still in its infancy.

Often we'll tell a publisher we need a PDF and they'll buy a program like Adobe Acrobat to convert to PDF. Then we receive the files and the customer doesn't have the experience or knowledge to embed the fonts properly or apply the correct resolution settings. This definitely delays the process significantly. Pretty consistently, the jobs are sliding back weeks at a time because we need to keep our production systems running. If a job is having issues, we will move it. We can't have a press standing idle.

If there is inexperience on the part of the self-publisher, it can end up being weeks lost before any issues are finally resolved and we are able to get to the next stage.

I blame ourselves to a certain extent. Perhaps in the sales process we didn't inquire enough about what their experience is and what type of files they'll be providing.

The absolute best way we like to receive files is in a PDF format. We, of course, work with the fundamental desktop publishing applications like Quark, InDesign, and PageMaker — the big publishing programs. The reason we prefer PDF is that our workflow system that we use to process files to plate, to prepare for printing, works with PDF. If you were to send me Quark files, we would run those Quark files and would preflight to the proofing process. But when we are ready to go to plate, we have to convert those into a PDF. With a PDF supplied, we've just eliminated a step out of our process.

Dealing with Corrections to the Files

With Quark, InDesign, Illustrator, and other programs, often we'll initiate changes for the customer during proofing. For example, I've sent you your blueline of the text and there are changes that are required — punctuation, adjustments here and there. Often the customer will have us make the changes to the application files, but we cannot make changes to the PDF. The customer will be required to make the changes to their source files from their end and then send us those new pages in PDF. We actually prefer that. We don't have a problem making changes for the customer, but there are charges with that. It's a billable process. A self-publisher will certainly save themselves some money by initiating changes themselves.

Another thing a lot of people don't consider is that if they're making the changes from their end, then their source files will be up-to-date and accurate. If we made the corrections from our end, the customer may not apply them to the original Quark files. Potentially, in the years to follow, you could run into a problem in regards to which version is the most up-to-date.

We can't physically change the PDF itself. You have to think of it as a hard copy of a document. Although it's electronic in format, it's not designed to be modified once it's been created. There are locks in place to keep it from being modified.

What our more experienced publishers do is provide us with both the source files and those files converted into PDF. Our workflow will default to using the PDF, but we will have the source Quark files on file. If there is a change that's required and they are unable to make the change at the customer side, we can go to the source file, make the correction, and then output to a PDF the pages that have changed. Then our archives contain all the updated files.

After fonts and image resolution problems, the next biggest problem is the quality of the material itself and how accurately it's been proofread, plus the volume of corrections that are required. We allocate a certain amount of time for proofing — about two to four days for a proof to be sent out, reviewed by the customer, marked up, and returned. If that time goes beyond four days, it will definitely delay our production schedule.

Perhaps there was some haste in providing the files and they weren't properly proofed prior to providing the files for output. I've received proofs back with pages of corrections, which could have been avoided. There is a cost involved with making the corrections and delays in having to proofread the blueline. This is opposed to having the blueline come back with six or seven corrections throughout the book. We make those corrections and do some remote proofing with the customer. Then we're into plating and production.

With our experienced publishers, you'd be surprised at how often we get no corrections coming back, or three or four. We can go to plating very quickly.

The Printing Process

When we receive the files, they automatically go into preflight. An operator will run the preflight software on them and do some manual checking, then provide me with a preflight report. That report is either going to say, "Okay, I can move that job to the next stage," or, "There are issues I need to communicate with the customer."

Once all the issues are resolved, the next stage is planning, which is basically allocation of stock, stock ordering, creating the impositions and layouts for that book to print on an offset press, ordering any special materials — for example, a hardcover that requires a foil stamp or dies — anything that is required for the physical production of the book.

Planning is actually a very quick process. It should occur within two days after preflight is complete.

Once planning is done, sometimes we will run into issues on something the customer has not confirmed, such as a certain type of material for the book. Perhaps they provided a general requirement but may not have specified a color, style, or material. That would come back to the customer service rep to resolve with the customer. Prior to getting to the preflight stage, know what you want.

Then our job goes into our prepress department. That's where the layout and pagination occur. We take the files and set them up as they would be required to run on the press, then output the proof. It would be as the book would be printed — the correct size, page count, margins. We send them out to the customer, and we're now into the proofing stage.

Delays in returning the proof will ultimately result in delays in the production of the book. There are incidents where we see proofs out for considerable periods of time. Anything that is out for more than a week is too long. If our production scheduling team sees proofs that are out for a week or more, you can bet your production date will be pushed around. There is too much riding on it. In order for us to be a successful business, our presses have to run continuously. If there are delays with one customer, another customer who does not have delays will be accelerated to fill that space. We'll do what we can to keep things on track, but delays do make things challenging and stressful. A customer who returns proofs quickly is in high regard.

Second-round proofing isn't always required. Sometimes, if there is just a minor correction to the copyright page, the customer may say they don't need to see another proof. With self-publishers, proofing can drag out. I've seen proofing go back and forth four or five times with multiple corrections. You can count on that delaying the production.

Proofing is finished and the files are signed off by the customer — in other words, everything is okay to print. At that point, we go to plating. The original plating process used film and all sorts of interesting processes to create plates. Now our PDFs are automatically processed through our plate-setters electronically. The key here is, after proofs are approved, the customer has no real time to make a change. Once we get that okay, we're going to plate. Then [if there are changes to be made] the customer has to decide, do you want to spend the extra $400 to get new plates done? It becomes expensive at that point, and it's guaranteed to delay your book because we have to go back to pagination, make all the corrections, re-output the PDF to the workflow, go back to proofing, and then back to plating again.

Once the plating phase is complete, your press time will be booked. That job will be run on the press, bound, trimmed, packed, and readied for shipping. In some degree, that is actually the quickest part of the process.

The time your book runs on a press depends on a number of factors: whether it's a color book or black-and-white, the press it's going to be running on, or the number of pages in the book (which will also determine the number of signatures required). When an offset press runs, we use sheets at presses. The pages need to be on one side of the sheet in an order that will allow those pages to be folded. Those signatures can be anywhere from 8 pages per signature (imagine a flat sheet with 8 pages on it) up to 48, depending on the size of the book. If you were to fold it a certain way, so that it now looks like one page, and you were to cut three sides of it, the pages would be in the correct order.

The size of a book determines the number of pages on a signature. The number of pages on a signature is directly related to the cost of the book. If you're doing a 12" x 12" book, you're not going to get more than 16 pages on a signature. Because of that, the cost of your book is going to increase.

The printing process is going to vary. We allocate a week for press and a week for binding and packing. Depending on the paper stock used, there is drying time required. We actually have to let the inks cure a little bit or you can end up with marking or smudging or bleeding on other pages. Some materials can take days. So two weeks for the actual production is allocated.

An offset press requires a lot of preparation to set up and a lot of time to run. The lower the quantity, the more time is spent for prepping and the less time actually running. For the higher quantities, if a press can run continuously for an extended period of time to run 3,000 to 4,000 copies, the price is going to come down. There are a lot of factors involved: size, type, colors — a lot of those factors will determine if it is more cost-effective on a digital or offset press. At about 750 copies, we start to ask our estimating department which way is more cost-effective. Anything under 750, we lean towards a digital run.

[When I asked why some printer quotes are so much higher than those from Friesens and other large book printers, Burton answered:]

As a company, we have a large number of presses and highly experienced staff. Other print shops may only have one press, so their production margins are probably a lot higher than ours are. In order for them to actually make a profit, they have to push that cost onto the customer.

Your Printer Is Your Partner

Self-publishers should ask as many questions as they need to be satisfied. At Friesens, we have a book called *A Guide to Book Production.* I'll often just send one out to a customer. If I get a call from somebody looking for a quote, just from the conversation, I can tell they are a self-publisher. I'll do the quote and without having them request it, I'll put a package together and send it out to them. There will be some things in there they need to know.

I would tell self-publishers to communicate their requirements with their printer. Consider your printer a partner in the production of your book. If you have a launch date, unusual shipping requirements, if the books are going to a specific retailer — any information like that in advance is going to allow the printer to work with them to meet those requirements. Communication is paramount.

8

It's All about Sales

As an expert in self-publishing, I've discovered three things that authors need to do:

1. Make sure your work is well edited for grammar, punctuation, and flow, so the reader is engaged from the beginning.

2. Invest in a good cover and professional text design. Looks are everything. You don't want your product to look like a self-published book.

3. Take action to market your book. Writing a book in itself will not make you rich. Sitting back just because your book is out there being advertised online or in a bookstore will not sell copies.

As this list emphasizes, before you can effectively market, you need to have a professional-looking product. It has to be something people will see the value in buying. It needs an attractive cover, good editing, and a purpose (e.g., entertainment, education, self-help, how-to).

However, you should be thinking about marketing and promotion before you even start writing the book, let alone editing or designing it. Try to presell as many books as you can. Your goal should be to sell enough books to fund the first print run. In order to do this, you need to put your marketing plan into action as soon as your outline is completed.

Pitch your book to the target market and come up with a unique angle.

When you develop a marketing plan you need to know the answers to the following questions (you'll recognize some of them from chapter 2):

- *Purpose*. What do you want your book to achieve? Why are you writing it?

- *Benefits*. The benefit of having a gas heating system is warmth on cold nights. What's the benefit of reading your book?

- *Audience*. Who is your audience? Don't say "everyone" because everyone doesn't care about your topic. What specific types of people or groups might be interested in the subject of your book?

- *Uniqueness*. What's your niche? What sets you apart from the rest of your competitors?

- *Action*. Who, what, when, where, how? Who will you approach? What will you say? When will you do it? Where are they located? How will you approach them?

- *Expertise*. Who are you? Why should they listen? What qualifies you to talk about this subject?

- *Budget*. How much will you spend to market your book? Advertising, bookmarks, flyers, direct mail packages, websites, brochures, postcards, greeting cards, calendars, trade shows, flea market tables can all help sell your book, but you will have to invest something to make it happen.

You also need to be persistent. Don't rest on your laurels when you've got into one outlet. Get the most value for the energy and money you expend.

In your marketing, pitch your book to the target market and come up with a unique angle. Every promotional piece you create should outline the benefits your reader will obtain by buying your book. Always remember, it's about the reader, not you.

It's about the Reader

The first thing you need to know is that not everyone will be interested in your book. Most of my self-published books are sports books, so unless an individual is interested in sports or sees the merit in purchasing the book as a gift for a sports fan in his or her family, that person is not going to care about the book or that I wrote it.

However, it doesn't matter that everyone isn't interested in my sports book. What I do know is that some people are. So when I prepare my marketing plan, I focus on the people who are more likely to buy my book.

Your goal is to determine who *will* be interested and how you will get them to buy your book. (Your bonus will be when they tell other people about it.) You also want to develop a readership that will wait anxiously to purchase your next book. Start by thinking about the following questions:

- Who are or will be your readers? Can you characterize them using specific descriptive terms? (If you've already published a book, who comes to your book signings, speaking engagements, and readings? Is there a commonality amongst them? Knowing more about your fan base will help you target your marketing message.)

- Why do people buy books? Why would someone be interested in your book?

- What other books are out there? Is your idea special? Is it unique? Check online to see if there is anyone else using the same angle as you. If you are writing a book to promote your business, how will it set you apart from, or ahead of, your competitors? What service can you offer in your book that will make people remember you? What valuable information are you sharing to ensure people will keep your book on their shelves for years to come?

- Do your books fit a theme? Can you define your book clearly and precisely, without having to go on for five minutes? You need to be able to show readers why your book is different and why they won't regret investing their time reading it.

Check online via Google, and at Amazon, Barnes & Noble, Borders, and Chapters/Indigo to see what books are similar to yours; then look for what sets yours apart from the rest. For example, my sports books look at professional sports from behind the scenes and try to inspire others with their stories. I would enter a phrase like "hockey or sports from behind the scenes" into search engines to look for similar books.

Only you can determine who your readers are. What are the demographics of the people who may be interested in your topic? If you don't know, you had better find out — perhaps by looking through bookstores and talking to booksellers about who buys that genre of book. In what section of the bookstore is it displayed? Is it a self-help book? Business book? Does it reach a home-based entrepreneur, parent, or youth worker? See what comes up when you Google the keywords.

How Do You Find Your Readers?

Once you know who your readers are and why they might be attracted to your book, you need to discover how to reach them. What magazines and newspapers do they read? What are their leisure activities? Where do they shop (both brick-and-mortar and online stores)? What websites do they visit?

Some of these things you will find out in the course of researching and writing your book. If you are writing a fantasy novel, you presumably enjoy reading fantasy and have some idea of what book clubs, Internet discussion groups, fan conventions, magazines, and other marketing opportunities are out there. If you are writing a book about archaeological digs around your city, you have probably been in touch with local archaeologists and educators (who might promote your book to interested people), and you likely are aware of what magazines, journals, and newsletters focus on this topic. For a hockey book, besides obvious markets like hockey teams and organizations, player associations, and fans, there are numerous venues in which a book could be marketed, such as sporting goods stores, development camps and hockey schools, and coaching organizations. Enter keywords related to your subject into an Internet search engine to see what other publications and groups come up.

If your book reaches an underserved market or taps into an inundated market with a refreshingly unique angle, you need to plan your marketing to capitalize on this potential.

Branding

You also need to figure out how to sell yourself. Along with the book, customers buy you; they buy your promises, your credibility, hope, stature, and success. If you establish yourself as an expert in the field you are writing about, people will clamor for your book.

This is what marketers call branding. Read about branding concepts on the Internet or in sales and marketing books and periodicals. Find examples of marketing firms that have helped people create their own brand. You are selling a book, not a company, but the principles are exactly the same. If your book or books present a theme, you can effectively brand yourself around that. For example, my brand is "Inspiring others through the positive message of sports." Once you've established a brand, you can better market to your target audience.

Of course, none of this happens overnight. This is something you should be working on long before your book even hits production.

It's about Sales, Too

Writing a book is all about sales. It doesn't matter what's between the covers if you can't sell it.

Like it or not, as a self-published author, *you* must become actively involved in selling your book. This is also true if you have placed a book with a traditional publisher. Perhaps the biggest myth in book publishing is that it's the publisher's job to sell the book, but as pointed out in chapter 4, publishers actively promote only a few books each year. Often, the most you can expect is for the publisher to send out a press release, list the book in its catalog or on its website, or do a one-shot advertisement. Depending on the scope of the book, the publisher may pay for a promotional tour.

As *Guerrilla Publicity* author Jill Lublin explains,

> I think the biggest misconception is you write a book and then you're finished. Ha! Actually, the work really begins once you've written the book.
>
> You've got to think about publicity. You've got to think about visibility. You've got to get the book seen and heard. Frankly, you can't stop. Most traditional publishers give it a six-week window of publicity. If you stop after six weeks, the sales of your book stop.
>
> After the success we made of *Guerrilla Publicity* and all our commitments to it and our publisher

saw what was happening, they asked me the great question, "What is your second book?" My second book's content came out of the fact that I am an excellent connector, am a great networker, and that I've been doing it naturally for years. I said, "Let's write the book *Networking Magic.*" Because we had done the work on *Guerrilla Publicity,* we really knew what to do with this one. It went number one on Barnes & Noble for three weeks in a row. It additionally has continued to sell well at Barnes & Noble, particularly displaying it on their end caps, with people seeing it all over the [United States] and Canada. We're enjoying great sales because of knowing what to do and how to do it fast.

Rob Lennard's book included some built-in elements to promote sales:

I did my marketing plan as I went along, but I've always been a good marketer. Writing a well-received centennial book in the year of Alberta's centennial was a huge help. I also had the foreword written by an NHL superstar, which created intrigue for the young readers. The prologue was written by the chief operating officer of one of Canada's finest museums, which provided excellent credibility for a historical fiction book.

Even Stan Fischler, who has seen most of his books produced by traditional publishers, advises, "I try to help as much as possible. You do what you can do. The author should get involved as much as possible."

What Is a Bestseller, Anyway?

In the United States, there is no set number of copies that must be sold in order for a book to be called a bestseller. The bestseller lists printed in newspapers and magazines are generated by certain booksellers for marketing purposes. These lists may include a variety of categories, such as hardcover fiction, hardcover nonfiction, trade paperback (softcover) fiction, trade paperback nonfiction, mass-market (pocket book) fiction, and mass-market nonfiction.

In Canada, a bestseller is a book that has sold 5,000 copies.

Sales 101

So how do you get your book to sell? It may be easier to start by listing some of the reasons a book *doesn't* sell:

Consider taking a sales course and learning as much as you can about marketing and sales.

- A book written for the author rather than the public will receive no attention or negative attention. Word will get around that it serves no purpose for the reader.

- Word will also get out if it's poorly written or doesn't have a good layout.

- A fabulously written and professionally presented book will not sell without a specific marketing plan that is followed through. Waiting for sales without active marketing is like waiting for the phone to ring when nobody knows you're dating.

- It won't sell if you're targeting the wrong audience.

- It also won't sell if you've targeted the right audience but haven't figured out how to reach it.

A well-marketed, well-produced book will sell. Aggressive authors who are able to get themselves noticed will see sales and a long shelf life for their book. So how do you get yourself and your book noticed?

- Consider taking a sales course and learning as much as you can about marketing and sales.

- Invest in a couple of good sales books. They will help you put your marketing plan into action. When I sold manufactured housing, Tom Hopkins' *How to Master the Art of Selling* was one of my two selling bibles. I loved his conversational style and the fact that I could translate his examples to whatever type of business I was in. The other book was Percy H. Whiting's *The 5 Great Rules of Selling.* He breaks his chapters down into easy-to-read points, which make it a handy reference book when you just want to check out one item, such as "rules for getting in." My newest bible is a self-published book by Wayne Clements, *The Selling Edge: A Consultative Approach.* His easy-to-read, commonsense approach is engaging, and his ideas are simple to incorporate. What you will notice when you read these three books is that their approach is timeless.

- Develop a marketing plan. You can use a shortcut available in the PowerPoint program. PowerPoint includes several templates that walk you through various aspects of business planning, including the marketing plan.

- Don't rely on word of mouth to sell your book. Tap your creative juices by always looking for opportunities.

- Many authors are introverted. They like sitting in a quiet room, thinking and writing. Many are not adept at sales or coming up with creative ideas. Take some time to evaluate your own attributes. Can you learn how to market effectively and like it? If not, maybe you should hire a marketer or publicist. Don't try to save on money if you know you're going to be too shy to pick up the phone and ask bookstores to stock your book, or to pitch yourself to the media.

- Promote yourself as more than just "the author of ..." This takes us back to branding, mentioned in the section "It's about the Reader." Establish yourself as an expert, someone readers can rely on to help them with problems or to entertain them. They'll be eager to buy your books.

- Use selling language in all your promotional material. See the next page for some examples taken from effective advertising.

- Hire a guerrilla marketer to come up with off-the-wall ideas for selling your book.

Getting Your Book into Bookstores

While it is possible for a self-publisher to actively solicit individual bookstores to carry his or her books, it is an onerous task, and generally, only local independent bookstores will choose to accept them. Bookstores do not usually deal with individual publishers. If they bought direct from publishers, they would end up with huge piles of invoices, one for each order from each publisher. Instead, they prefer to consolidate their bookkeeping by ordering from a distributor.

The Distributor

A distributor may represent hundreds, even thousands, of publishers. It will sell to the major book chains, big-box stores, and online markets as well as to independent bookstores across North

Language That Sells

The following are words and phrases you can use in your advertising materials to draw attention to your book. In advertising, as with the book cover, you only have a few seconds to grab someone's attention. The best way to do that is to make the advertising about the reader, to show how he or she will benefit — this is why these words are so powerful.

Persuasive phrases:

Yours free (e.g., advice, tips)

Money-making facts — Free

News: Just arrived

Just off the press

It's here

Top ten words used in advertising that capture people's attention:

You	Who	Now
Your	Money	Why
How	People	New
Want		

Most persuasive words:

Announcing	Amazing	Revolutionary
Miracle	Quick	Compare
Suddenly	Introducing	Sensational
Startling	Challenge	Wanted
Bargain	Now	Improvement
Remarkable	Magic	Offer
Easy	Hurry	

Words that denote news:

Announcing	Introducing	Presenting
Today	New	Now
Novel	Modern	Recent
Latest	Suddenly	Revolutionary

America. Having a distributor gives your book more credibility. It also provides you with a sales force and fulfillment center.

The two biggest buying periods in the book industry are spring and fall. A few months before each season starts (i.e., in June/July for the fall and Christmas season, and in February/March for the spring), a distributor will create a catalog of new titles, and its sales representatives will make sales calls to bookstores, present the list of new books, and take orders. The sales reps use tip sheets, cover art, buy sheets, and book samples to sell the distributor's inventory to the bookstores. You will want to make sure your book is ready in time for one of these seasons. If it falls in between the major selling periods, you will lose sales. However, you should also remember that your book isn't the only book the distributor and its reps are selling.

The distributor warehouses the inventory and ships books to each bookstore as ordered. Bookstores order from the distributor on a returnable basis. Returns are sent back to the distributor *at the publisher's expense* — over and above the 20 percent the distributor takes for each book sale. While terms vary, bookstores generally take 40 percent of the retail price and the distributor receives 20 percent of the retail price. From the balance (40 percent), the publisher pays the author royalties (generally 10 percent); the remaining 30 percent must cover production costs, overhead, marketing, shipping, etc.

How long a book remains on the shelves depends on how well the book sells, which can depend on the author's involvement in the sales effort. Keep in mind the industry average: half of the books you see on bookstore shelves will be sent back to the distributor, then to the publisher. For this reason, distributors keep a reserve fund. They hold back some of the money they owe the publisher (usually about 10 percent) to cover the cost of future returns.

Sometimes, rather than return books, booksellers will discount the price to encourage sales. Occasionally the more popular books are discounted in order to bring more people into the store and create more sales, but often the discounted books are the ones that aren't selling. If a book is discounted and ends up on the bargain table, it means the distributor's, the publisher's, and the author's share are discounted accordingly. This fact may be disturbing, but a discount sale is still better than a return. Personally, I'd rather sell 1,000 books at $10 than 250 books at $25.

A distributor will decide whether or not to carry your book based on your outline (see chapter 2). It may also ask you to send a copy of your book (which means you have to make the commitment and print copies of your book before you know for sure that you have a distributor for it).

To be accepted by a distributor, your book must not only fit the editorial direction of the company (some distributors handle specific genres), but also be professionally presented. It must be saddle-stitched or perfect-bound — no spiral bindings unless you've published a cookbook. (Note: Distributors don't accept print-on-demand books.) Your book will need a bar code, an ISBN, and a reasonable, competitive price. It helps if you have a marketing plan.

Distributors must be convinced that the book will appeal to the general marketplace. In other words, they have to be convinced the book will make money. Distributors make their money from book sales, so if they don't believe a book is salable, they won't take it on.

Getting a distributor is not an easy task. It can be as difficult as finding a traditional publisher. Many distributors are owned by major publishing houses and will only work with other major publishers, but there are some companies that specialize in independent and self-publishers.

One important thing to realize is that once your book starts selling to bookstores, you are unlikely to see any of the money

If you have signed a contract with a distributor, you still should promote your own book.

from these sales until at least three months later. This quashes another myth about book publishing — if you just get your book into a bookstore, you can count your millions. In reality, it takes a long time to get paid.

Another thing you need to know is that your contract with a distributor is usually exclusive. If you sign up with a company that distributes to the United States only, you will need to find another distributor that operates in Canada, but if your first distributor works with bookstores in both countries, you cannot approach another distributor without breaching the contract (unless the first distributor agrees to handle sales in only one country). There are some small distributors that deal exclusively in one state or province. You may want to sign with such a company if you can't get a national distributor or if your book is likely to sell only in that state or province. However, you could lose a deal with a national distributor if you've already signed a contract for a state/province-wide distributor unless you can find a way to terminate that arrangement.

Finally, before you sign, check the distribution contract to see a list of the distributor's retail outlets other than bookstores. It will likely include major retailers like Wal-Mart, Costco, Safeway, and Amazon. These and any other retailers mentioned in your distribution contract are out of bounds for you. If you are thinking of doing some selling outside the bookstores, you can't sell to these stores. What you can do, however, is make these outlets, and even bookstores, aware of your product, but direct them to order from your distributor. In fact, I highly recommend that you do visit stores periodically to talk up your book. Your book may be overlooked when it's just one of hundreds in the distributor's catalog, but the personal touch will make it stand out for the retailer. (It's especially good to drop in to let bookstores or other retailers know when there is going to be some publicity about you or the book. This will give them a chance to ensure they have copies on hand when people come in looking for the book after they've read about it in the paper or heard you speak on the radio.)

As with anything else, you may need to try out a distributor for a period of time, but if, after six months, your arrangement isn't working, you should find out why and move on. Of course, lack of sales may not be the distributor's fault. It could be your book. Perhaps the booksellers do not see any merit in ordering it and can't picture it selling in their stores. If that is the case, your distributor should tell you, whether you want to hear it or not.

Beware when you are seeking a distributor. Just as there are disreputable agents, there are a lot of illegitimate distributors out there who will try to charge you an unreasonable amount of money for either a catalog advertisement or administration fee. Do your homework. See who that distributor is representing, then contact a few of those publishers to see if they are satisfied with the service. If you have signed up with a distributor and haven't heard anything from it for several months, contact some of the other publishers on its list. (You can find out what other publishers a distributor carries by checking its website or catalog.) If the distributor isn't doing its job, there is usually a termination clause in the contract. You may only need to send a letter to terminate the agreement. The contract will indicate what action you need to take.

Online Bookstores — Amazon and Others

Amazon.com is one of the biggest names in the bookselling industry, and the Amazon Advantage Program is available to anyone who has published a book. Whether or not you have landed a distributor, you can still list your title on Amazon by clicking onto the website and allowing the prompts to walk you through the process. This gives you an online presence, and if you're doing a media interview, or if potential buyers live outside your jurisdiction, you can suggest they buy your book from Amazon rather than trying to contact you directly and dealing with checks or money orders.

While Amazon pays promptly for books sold and keeps good records that you can access online, it doesn't carry a large inventory of any book and may order only one, two, or three at a time. Because of this, it can cost the same as your earnings to mail or courier these books to Amazon. That's why, if you do get a distributor, you want to turn over your Amazon account to them right away. Distributors normally have a list of Amazon orders for several books and send them all at the same time. It's a much more cost-effective option.

Another option, if you don't have a national distributor, is to look into listing your book on the Barnes & Noble website, <www.bn.com>. There are several other online bookstores, but many of them are already linked to Amazon or Barnes & Noble.

Getting into Bookstores without a Distributor

Without a distributor, you can still get your books into bookstores with a little elbow grease. You could ask the store manager to test your book by placing it in a high-traffic area to see if it generates interest. Arm yourself with reviews and any special marketing and promotion plans to show that you are taking an active role in selling your book. You will likely have to offer a complimentary copy of the book to the manager so he or she can decide if the book is salable. One author who got his books into a store paid to ensure his books appeared on the end shelves of one of the store's aisles. He made his money back almost overnight due to the high exposure.

Fred Gleeck, the author of *Publishing for Maximum Profit,* <www.selfpublishingsuccess.com>, suggests a reverse shoplifting technique. Leave three or four copies of your book in the relevant section of a bookstore. When someone picks up a copy and goes to buy it, the bookseller will realize it's not in the system. Rather than turning away the customer, the seller will try to find a way to process the sale. Gleeck's idea is if bookstores start selling the book, they'll want to place an order with the distributor or publisher.

An independent New York publisher tried a distribution concept similar to that used by Columbia House records and some of the book clubs. The publisher would e-mail a list of titles to the bookstores. Unless stores specifically declined any or all titles, the publisher would send them two copies, with an invoice offering the standard discount. Every season he sent two copies of his titles to everyone who signed up until he was told not to. Of course, he would also accommodate those who asked for extra copies. The risk in this type of marketing is you are stuck with the cost of mailing copies of books with no guarantee of remuneration.

While books are usually accepted on a consignment basis, some authors have successfully managed to sell their books on a non-returnable basis by offering an attractive discount. As a self-publisher, you have control over the discount you offer on your books. Often I will offer a consignment discount (the industry average of 40 percent) and a buyout discount, which allows stores to purchase the books outright for much less. It creates an instant sale and *no returns.*

Lyle Manery remembers when he started publishing his books:

> There were lots of independent bookstores and it
> was relatively easy to place books on consignment.
> It took a lot of legwork. You need to see the man-
> ager at his or her convenience. For more distant
> locations, it is best to contract a distributor.

Ron and Adrianna Edwards agree:

> [Getting into bookstores] is one of the most diffi-
> cult parts of the whole publishing process and one
> of the reasons traditional publishers can demand 90
> percent of the cover price (okay, over 40 percent
> goes to the retailer). Amazon, etc., certainly help
> make this easier, but it is still tough. As someone
> said, there is a lot of noise out there, and it is
> nearly impossible to stand out from the crowd. Be
> creative.

For each book that successfully reaches a bookstore, there are
many more that do not. In your book's business plan, prepare to
solicit a distributor, but plan for sales outside the bookstore. In
Warren Redman's opinion, that may be better than getting into
bookstores anyway:

> Bookstores are not my favorite place for [selling]
> books. Most want them on consignment, some
> take many months to pay, or return unsold books.

Think Outside the (Big) Box or Independent

Consider income from the bookstores as gravy, and don't judge the
success of your marketing on signing with a distributor or having
your book in bookstores. Search for ideas outside the norm —
think outside the box.

Wholesaling

Look for opportunities to wholesale your book, even if it means
selling each copy for barely more than the cost of printing. If you
sell a lot of books at that price, it can add up to more than if you

sell fewer books at a higher price. Wal-Mart uses this approach to retailing. Wal-Mart pays vendors extremely low prices for the goods it sells, but vendors make money because the chain buys in bulk.

There are a number of creative ways to achieve sales outside the bookstores:

- A business book could be offered to a professional group (e.g., accountants) or members (individuals or companies) of an industry association.

- A sports book could be sold in sporting goods stores.

- An evangelical book could be sold by churches.

- Lawyers who specialize in divorce could sell a book on mediation to clients.

- Accountants could sell a book on how to beat the taxman.

- Real estate agents could sell books on winterizing your home or readying your house for selling.

- Mechanics or car dealerships could offer their customers books showing them easy and inexpensive ways to maintain their cars.

- Professional speakers can sell their books at the back of the room when they give keynote speeches or lead workshops.

- Musicians can sell their books alongside T-shirts at their concerts.

- Professional athletes can do book signings at team community events, offering a percentage to charity.

- Actors can have their books available for sale at theatres.

- Talk show hosts and media can promote their books during their shows.

- Flea markets or other types of specialty markets are possible venues. (I would suggest attending the market first to see how tables are set up and to learn how the best vendors get attention. You'll discover there is an art to their presentation.)

- Gift stores and specialty shops are other possible venues (although if you have a distributor, you'll need to make sure these types of stores aren't covered in the contract).

- Restaurants, Welcome Wagon, real estate agents, and housing developers may want to buy your book in bulk to sell, or possibly give, to clients.

Your sales opportunities are only limited by your imagination.

- Nonprofit organizations, service clubs, or professional associations might be interested in buying your book in bulk to sell to members (if the topic is relevant to their community) or for fundraising ventures. For example, local schools and community groups are always looking for ways to raise money. You can offer your books at cost (say $5) for them to sell at retail price (maybe $15 or $20). The school or group would then earn $10 or $15 for every book sold. Alternatively, you can sell the books as part of a program where you offer a percentage of sales to benefit an event that the schools or groups want sponsored. In this situation, you still need to do the selling, but presumably students and teachers or group members will be talking about your book, trying to increase sales in order to earn money for their project.

- Businesses might want to buy several boxes of books to use as gifts for customers if the subject is related to their business. For example, a nursery may buy a few hundred copies of your gardening book.

- There may be book clubs or other mail-order catalogs that would offer your book for sale to members.

- Don't rule out places like the military and schools, although you'll need to check out their vendor requirements.

The list goes on and on. Your sales opportunities are only limited by your imagination. Here are a few more marketing ideas:

- Keep a database of the names and addresses of people you were in touch with during your research and let them know when the book comes out. They will likely want a copy for themselves and may have ideas of other potential buyers. (Note: If you relied on one or two people for a lot of information, you should give them a complimentary copy of your book as a thank-you.) If you've written a book with tips or self-help advice, you may have included information provided by other people. Perhaps you ran an ad in your local paper, asking people for suggestions on gardening in your city or the best places to shop. If you credited your contributors by

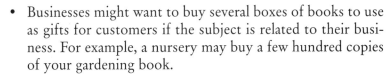

name, they'll line up to buy a copy — and will talk up your book to their friends.

- Send out publication announcements to trade newsletters, business groups, and e-mail lists. Include information on ordering your book and indicate that you offer discounts for bulk purchases. Suggest ways companies and groups can make money using your book — they may not think of it on their own, but if you spell it out, you're making it easy for them to follow through (see Sample 7 in the "Direct Mail" section of this chapter).

- Offer to donate a book to an organization for a contest or as an item for a charity auction. This earns you some goodwill and also brings your book to the attention of a wider audience of potential buyers.

- You can print your book cover on T-shirts, bumper stickers, postcards, bookmarks, mouse pads, calendars, greeting cards, or mugs, and use these to market your book. Choose items that people are unlikely to throw out, as they keep your book in sight and in their minds. Make sure you include contact information, particularly your website or e-mail address, so people can find you. On some of these items you can also include tips and ideas that will plant a seed in people's memories.

- At the very least, make sure your book cover is on your business cards, envelopes, and maybe even letterhead and invoices. Here's a tip for getting the most from the money you pay for printing. Ask the printer if there is any gutter space left on the sheet. If there is, find out how much you have to work with. It doesn't cost the printer anything to run something else in the gutter — for example, bookmarks or business cards, even a smaller booklet. It may cost extra to cut it out, but any time you place a print order, keep that in the back of your mind. Is there room to run something else on the sheet?

- I included a survey at the back of my book, *Inside the NHL Dream*. It asked for readers' opinions on the book's topic, what stories they liked best, if the book met their expectations, and what other books they'd like to see in the future. Even more than two years after it was released, I still get amazing feedback.

- You might start an electronic newsletter or magazine and offer subscribers a discount on your next book.

- When your book is laid out, make sure you include an order form at the back, not only for that book, but also for other books you've published.

- A book that's selling well will generate more sales (this is the theory behind bestseller lists). If you can announce you've sold several hundred copies in one week, or that you're down to your final 100 copies, people who haven't bought your book will think they're missing out on something important. (But see the "Stay Ethical" section later in this chapter— don't make these claims if they're not true or people will view you, and your book, as a fraud.) If your self-published book is doing well, you may find there are traditional publishers interested in republishing it.

Libraries

If you have applied for CIP data for your book (see chapter 6), it will automatically be included in lists of new books which are distributed to booksellers and libraries before the book is published. That means you could possibly receive an unsolicited order from a library somewhere in the country.

Actively marketing to libraries can be lucrative, but it takes some work to compile a list of contacts for every library in the country or throughout North America. You can purchase mailing lists for school, public, and specialty libraries, but this information is also available online. My philosophy has always been not to pay for information that is available elsewhere at no charge and is also likely more up-to-date, although it may take time to find it. Visit Libweb <lists.webjunction.org/libweb> or PublicLibraries.com <www .publiclibraries.com>, which list links to library directories from the United States and many other countries, or the Canadian Library Gateway <www.collectionscanada.ca/gateway>, which provides information on Canadian libraries. You might also find information at your local library. Call the reference librarian and ask where you would find contact information for the type of library you want to approach. I remember the years before the Internet (was there such a time?) when I practically lived in the reference section of the library, and there are still many print directories there that are a goldmine of information (though perhaps not always as up-to-date as websites).

The more interviews you can arrange, the better.

Trade Shows and Meetings

No matter what your book is about, there is probably some association or alliance of groups interested in the topic, and that association may hold an annual meeting or a trade show. This offers you an opportunity for speaking engagements (see chapter 9) and a chance for you to sell your book.

Partnerships

There are numerous types of partnerships you can generate before and after your book is in print. You can partner with organizations that will do the following:

- Buy or presell your books as corporate gifts
- Sponsor the cost of printing in return for significant recognition (e.g., a credit inside the book or on the cover)
- Use your book as an educational textbook (if appropriate)
- Feature your book on their website — in exchange, they'll likely expect you to highlight their organization or books on your website
- Use your book as a fundraiser
- Reach the same target audience

When looking for a partnership, as you would do when seeking a traditional publisher or a distributor, find an organization that will be a good fit. Make a case for a win-win arrangement. Most organizations don't care that you wrote a book. They want to know why they should participate and what's in it for them. If there isn't a benefit for both parties, they're likely to decline getting involved.

Advertising

Your book is your advertising. If you've done a good job on the cover, have a good title, and have written a compelling description on the back, you enhance your marketing capabilities tenfold just by having it in a location where people can see it.

Publicity is also advertising. The more interviews you can arrange (on television, radio, or in print media), the better — because they're free. See chapter 9 for more on getting publicity.

You may also decide to purchase advertising. Advertising is expensive, and a one-shot ad rarely works. Many businesses make the mistake of putting all their eggs in one advertising basket, blowing their whole budget on one glitzy ad in a well-known publication. Unfortunately, such ads often don't generate a single call. For advertising to work, it must be repetitive. A seed is planted with the first ad. The second ad starts working on the subconscious. The third ad might be the one that gets noticed by those who are in the market for your product.

When you are planning an ad campaign, keep the following points in mind:

- Use a professional designer. Advertising is an art. A poorly designed ad will turn people off. If the ad looks amateurish, they'll assume your book is also unprofessional.

- Keep the text clear and concise, but make sure you include the main selling points of your book. Proofread it. Proofread it again!

- Be sure to include all your contact information so interested people are able to get hold of the book. (You'd be surprised how many people miss this step.)

- If you don't have a lot of money to spend, make sure you choose the one or two best outlets to reach your target market. Your ad can be overlooked in publications like the local newspaper or general consumer magazines.

- You might pre-advertise in targeted publications for two reasons: to get some prepublication orders and to plant seeds (i.e., putting the word out that your book is on its way so people will recognize it when it is eventually released). However, don't let this be your only venue. Many people won't buy a book till they can see it. Even if their interest is piqued by an ad, they may have forgotten about it by the time the book appears.

Having a Web Presence

If you don't have a website, get one. It may not sell many books, but it does give you credibility and a place to post more information about yourself, your business, and your book. Be sure to let visitors know where they can find the book (e.g., which bookstores or retail outlets; on Amazon.com; through local schools, churches, or nonprofit groups). I suppose even a bad website is better than none, but like a real estate agent's car, your website design reflects your professionalism.

Plan your website as if it were a new business. What is its purpose? What message do you want to send? What will people take away from it? What might draw people back to visit or inspire them to refer it to other people? Do your homework. Check out other sites that appeal to you. What elements work? Do they have contests or games?

Create your own text and make sure the information is proofed and corrected before it is posted online. Web designers may think they are writers, but how many websites have you visited where you spotted more than the usual number of spelling and grammar errors? Use the PowerPoint business plan to walk you through the process of planning your website.

Try to have a presence on some of the websites your target audience is visiting. Post a message in the discussion forums on these websites. Don't blatantly advertise your book (that's a quick way to get booted out of the forum). Instead, post a tip or comment that will inform the reader about a related topic.

Include a signature block at the end of every e-mail you send out. It should identify you as "Author of ..." and give your contact information. If writing is your business, you are doing yourself a disservice by not adding a signature to your e-mails. (Check the help file of your e-mail program for instructions on creating a signature.)

Offer to write an online article — again, not advertising your book. What this does is set you up as an expert. Specifically target web publications that reach your preferred audience. Whether or not you are paid for your writing, you are making an impression on that marketplace. Your bio will say "Author of ..." and have a link to your website. If you offer value, you'll create an interest. If you're just writing to promote yourself and flog your wares, most readers will tune out and click on the next article.

As an alternative to writing a new article, you can also look for opportunities to post excerpts of your book on other websites and in newsletters. Most of the larger corporations are always looking for content for their internal newsletters.

Search regularly for more online venues to work with. Websites are like restaurants. Some establish a presence and loyal customer base; others drop out of sight before the next wholesale order.

Find other like-minded websites and trade links. Start with people in your own circle of influence. The Internet can be a great tool for marketing, but you have to take the time to look for the right opportunity. Sponsored sites on search engines, such as Google, give you better placement. (When you access the Google search engine, you'll see the sponsored links listed on the right-hand side. You pay a minimal amount each time someone clicks on your sponsored link. Depending whether you are listed first, second, or third, the rate you pay will vary.) Rather than targeting searches about writing or publishing, target the searches relating to your book's topic.

Direct Mail

In the days before e-mail, marketers would send out bulk mailings containing information about their products, hoping to entice people to buy. You may still have occasion to do this, but postage has become expensive. In the United States, the cost of mailing a first-class letter within the country starts at $0.37, which adds up in a hurry. If you're going to use postage mail, be particular about who you target. You may want to mail postcards or bookmarks with your book cover to the people you most want to impress — people you already know.

Today, with the immediacy and scope of the Internet, you can reach a lot of more people for a minimal investment of money. But who do you target?

For a start, as you research your book, be sure to file the contact information for any people you interview or receive information from, as well as any groups or individuals you discover who have an interest in the topic. You may find more potential buyers as you prepare your marketing plan. These are the people you will approach through direct mail. There are numerous directories of membership lists available online, and there are certainly mailing lists you can purchase for a premium. For example, a magazine may sell you its subscriber list if your book is one its subscribers might be interested in. When it comes to finding lists, you have to roll up your sleeves and go online to seek out any site that offers a potential

Sometimes it only takes one complaint to your Internet service provider about spam to have them cancel your e-mail address and/or website.

fit. The more specific you are in the terms you enter in a search engine, the more exact your target list will be.

Create an e-mail template of your book information, which you can send out to different people with slight variations. Recipients are more inclined to read your e-mail if you've taken the time to personalize it, which you can do by typing "Dear [Individual's Name]" in the appropriate place and sending the e-mail to them alone. This may take a little more time than simply sending out a blanket, generic e-mail, but the results are much greater. Sample 7 shows an e-mail flyer that can easily be customized.

Sending one e-mail out to hundreds of people at the same time may not be effective anyway. Unsolicited commercial e-mail is considered to be spam. You are at risk of being accused of spamming if you indiscriminately send out e-mails in bulk, especially if you use the regular "To" box on your e-mail. Many servers will assume that e-mails with hundreds of addresses in the "To" box are spam and will reject them. Spam filters may also kick in, depending on what you use for a subject line.

If the server does let non-personalized e-mails through, some recipients become irritated when they have to scroll through those hundreds of addresses. People in your address book might take exception to having their e-mail addresses displayed for everyone else to see in the "To" box, and unhappy e-mail recipients are unlikely to buy books. Even using the "Bcc" (blind carbon copy) e-mail address box — which hides all the e-mail addresses from view — may put you at risk of being labeled a spammer, particularly if you are sending unsolicited mail out on a weekly basis. Recipients who aren't interested will use their software filters to block all messages from your address, but you could experience a worse fate. Sometimes it only takes one complaint to your Internet service provider about spam to have them cancel your e-mail address and/or website.

When you send out a large number of e-mails, whether they're generic or personalized, make sure you empty your Sent and Trash mailboxes frequently to free up cyberspace storage, because once you reach a certain quota, your e-mails will start to bounce. Some will bounce anyway due to other people's mailboxes being full or because you have incorrect or defunct addresses. What you don't want is to have your mailbox too full to send any more e-mails or to receive responses — especially orders!

SAMPLE E-MAIL FLYER

Freelance Communications
123 Main Street
My Town, AB T3E 3H4
(403) 240-1340; (403) 249-4249 Fax
freelancecommunications@shaw.ca or delicksen@shaw.ca
www.freelancepublishing.net

October 1, 20--

Dear_____:

Because of your commitment to your clients and their lifestyles, you may already recognize
and support the inherent benefits sport brings to our communities. This is the reason I'm writing
to you.

My books offer others the principles of success through the venue of sport. They show that
in life, there is no free lunch. Hard work and persistence are the keys to developing talent and
making dreams possible.

Future Prospects (ISBN 0-9730237-4-0, 2005) has the blessing of Ron Robison, the commissioner
of the Western Hockey League, who has also written the foreword. It's a behind-the-scenes look
at the lifestyle of major junior hockey from both current and former junior and National Hockey
League players such as Kelly Hrudey, Richard Zednik, Jarome Iginla, Mike Modano, Mike Ricci,
Jacques Lemaire, Ethan Moreau, and Alex Tanguay, to name a few.

Positive Sports: Professional Athletes and Mentoring Youth (ISBN 0-9730237-3-2, 2003) shows
the giving side of professional sports and how it has a lasting impact on our communities. It
features Vince Carter, Mark McLoughlin, Jayson Krause, Shareef Abdur-Rahim, Juwan Howard,
and Doug Gilmour, among others. I was told by a friend that this book had made the "must read"
list at the Admissions Conference in Toronto.

Inside the NHL Dream (ISBN 0-9730237-0-8, 2002) looks at what happens behind the scenes in
the National Hockey League, from trades, travel, time commitments, and family sacrifices to the
physical toll and what it's like to live on the bubble. Personalities such as Jarome Iginla, Paul
Kariya, James Patrick, Perry Berezan, and Kelly Hrudey are featured, among many others. When
I did the interviews for this project, Kelly Hrudey and others stopped me several times during the
course of the interview to say how much they thought it was about time someone took this angle.
The feedback has been extremely positive from both inside and outside NHL circles.

These books could be used as gifts for your clients, as a fundraiser for amateur sports and youth
organizations, for programs such as youth reading initiatives (for example, Reading — Give It a
Shot), and for distribution to minor sports or youth organizations and hospitals.

The costs of these books through Freelance Communications are:

- US$12.00/CDN$15.00 retail per book
- US$10.00/CDN$12.00 for 10 to 20 books
- US$320.00/CDN$350.00 per box of 54 (includes delivery)
- US$2.46/CDN$3.00 per book for 2,000+

I'm hoping you will consider using these as gifts for your clients or a community venture. FYI, the San Jose Sharks have opted to promote *Future Prospects* to their season ticket holders, and the Wyoming Amateur Hockey Association is distributing the book to its development camps.

I look forward to partnering with you in spreading a positive message about sports.

Sincerely,

Debbie Elicksen

Freelance Communications provides support to self-publishers who want to market themselves through books.

***

FUTURE PROSPECTS

Take a tour inside the lifestyle of major junior hockey from the players' perspective

***

INSIDE THE NHL DREAM

A hockey book unlike any other — take a tour of the national hockey league from the inside

As seen on *Hockey Night in Canada*, the NHL Network, and *The Vicki Gabereau Show*

Available in bookstores throughout the United States and Canada

***

POSITIVE SPORTS: PROFESSIONAL ATHLETES AND MENTORING YOUTH

Positive Sports was highlighted as a "must read" at the Admissions Conference in Toronto in the fall of 2003.

Available in bookstores throughout the United States and Canada (also search in Google Print)

Lyle Manery says:

> Direct marketing has been quite successful for me. Two years ago, I went to an organization and, through them, sent out a mailing to over 15,000 other members. That project garnered sales of 444 sets of books. There were five books to a set. Last year, I did an e-mail broadcast to the same group. The results were lower, but still reasonable — 254 sets of five books.

Networking

Never underestimate the power of networking. People like to support and do business with the people they know, and networking is the art of making and using contacts.

One of the most effective ways of marketing a business is through networking. However, many people misunderstand networking and how to use it. It isn't about walking into an event and trying to sell your product to anyone who will listen. It's about developing relationships. You should always have books handy in the trunk of your car or your briefcase, just in case, but being in people's faces and pressuring them to buy does not win friends. Use the techniques mentioned below, whether you are selling to friends, colleagues, or strangers.

- Look at your circle of influence from both a business and personal perspective. Who do you know? Where do they work? Who do they know?

- Join business groups or organizations whose members are the people you want to meet. If you want to connect with the business community, joining a writing group will not help you achieve that. Join the chamber of commerce instead.

- Develop a relationship with the people you've interviewed by sending them a thank-you card with a copy of the book's proposal.

- Meet as many people as you can. Look at every gathering as a potential networking event. Don't go to a party and walk up to the first person you see and try to sell him or her a book. Work the crowd. Mingle. Be interested in the other people who are there. If they like what you do, they will show their interest. That is when you can think about exchanging cards.

Networking is the most powerful tool you can use to get noticed.

- When you network, never walk into a room expecting to take something away without giving something first. Note that the person you talk to first may not be an individual you need to connect with, but by engaging in conversation and finding out who he or she is, you may discover that his or her brother, sister, uncle, or co-worker could be a person you need to see.

- If you receive someone's card, follow up. Send them a quick e-mail or note to say how nice it was to meet them. Or send then an article or tidbit of information from a newspaper or the Internet on a subject that you think might interest them. That's what networking is — making a connection, creating a personal inventory of people who will become your "disciples" (people who tell others how great you are).

Networking is the most powerful tool you can use to get noticed. But it doesn't happen overnight. Making strong relationships takes time, but if you make the effort to do this, you'll never regret it. You'll be amazed at how small the world will become.

Here are some tips on how to network:

1. Meet as many people as you can.

2. Tell people what you do.

3. Introduce yourself (act like a host, not a guest).

4. Don't do business while networking (set up a meeting for later).

5. Give (do favors) in order to get (someday you may need a favor yourself). Do volunteer work.

6. Follow up (this is when you'll do your business).

7. Keep in touch.

8. Make friends (even if you think you don't need them).

9. Edit your contacts annually (weed out those people or companies that are non-productive or a poor fit).

Use whatever it takes to open a door. If you want to be known, you have to be seen. Look at politicians. They are gold medalists at schmoozing and networking. They know exactly who their audience is, where to spend their time, and how to ask for what they want.

Lyle Manery describes a positive networking experience he was involved with:

> The most successful marketing story that I can relate from firsthand knowledge is about a cookbook. Two ladies joined our self-publishing organization and asked for a general critique of the book and their plans for it. The entire group participated and freely shared our collective knowledge and experience. It was an exhilarating event for everyone. There were many imaginative suggestions including some that were later incorporated. These ladies went on to sell over 750,000 cookbooks. Their experiences and successes inspired them to form a business that is now helping a growing number of authors to publish and promote their books. It was a thrill to be part of this great success story.

Stay Ethical

Don't think you can influence book sales by unethical means. Word gets around fast in the bookselling industry. Placing false orders to trump up sales figures in bookstores, and any attempt to get a bookseller to order extra quantities of nonreturnable books will get you blacklisted in a heartbeat. The source can always be traced. You also risk legal consequences. Why would you want to chance throwing away your career as an author?

Another ruse that will backfire on you is if you arrange a book signing with an independent bookstore without any intention of keeping your commitment, hoping that your sales will be boosted by the extra books that the store ordered for your signing.

You'll hear about people trying to manipulate the Amazon bestseller list by having everyone they know buy the book within a 24-hour period. Trying to trick the Amazon system will also blacklist you.

Some authors will even misrepresent the content of their book to increase sales.

There's no substitute for ethical and acceptable marketing practices.

The Bottom Line

When you are selling your book, think of the intangible elements of what you are offering. What are you really selling? Hope, inspiration, business tools, entertainment, a reality check?

Nobody buys a book because it's there. They buy it because it will offer them something they need, something they can glean ideas from, something that will help them get through a rough patch in their lives. Always keep this in mind when you look for ways to market your book.

9

Getting Noticed on a Larger Scale

Publicity and marketing go hand in hand. You plan publicity as part of your marketing plan, but the beauty of publicity is that some of it will come to you without your having to reach for it. Publicity uses the media and public platforms to get noticed. Publicity can beget publicity if you plan well.

Peer Reviews/Testimonials

Peer reviews and testimonials are the blurbs you see on the covers of books or in promotional copy on websites:

> "This is the greatest novel I've ever read!"
>
> — Famous author

or

> "Tells you everything you ever wanted to know about installing new plumbing fixtures."
>
> — Home renovator with a popular TV show

Testimonials provide positive comments on the book's contents. They are written by famous people or by experts who may not be as well known, but whose position or publishing credits (which are included with the blurb) give them credibility.

Awards can be a form of testimonial, especially if they come from an organization with credibility in the book's subject area.

Do these testimonials work?

Ron and Adrianna Edwards think so:

> They work particularly well for academic-type books, but there is a lot of competition out there and only so many recognizable names to endorse your book.

One of my clients e-mailed the first few chapters of his book to several customers and individuals whose opinion he valued. He asked them to read the chapters, then send him a paragraph to let him know what they thought about the material and if they would recommend the book to others. In return for submitting a review, he promised them an autographed copy as a thank-you once the book was published. The response to his request was overwhelming, and he was able to include three full pages of reviews at the front of his book.

Another woman, who wrote a book on a health care issue, circulated her manuscript to, and solicited input from, several well-known doctors who were concerned with this particular health issue. She successfully asked them to endorse her book both within their associations and in testimonials. One of the doctors also wrote the foreword. Sample 8 shows a covering letter you could use to request testimonials.

Awards can be a form of testimonial, especially if they come from an organization with credibility in the book's subject area. Warren Redman, author of *The 9 Steps to Emotional Fitness,* says,

> One of the more successful boosts to my latest book was the Best Book Award it won from the Canadian Counselling Association. Winning an award gave it better credibility than any testimonial could have.

Book Events

Book signings, book readings, BookExpo (the national booksellers' trade fairs in the United States and Canada) — there are several events you can organize or take part in to promote your book and let people know that it's available. It's all about getting noticed. The more you're "out there," the more people will hear about you and your book.

SAMPLE 8
SAMPLE LETTER REQUESTING TESTIMONIALS

July 1, 20--

U.R. Expert
4499 Poplar Road
Big Town, WA 94449

Dear Mr. Expert:

Please find attached a copy of the first three chapters from my book *Self-Publishing for Everyone*, which will be published this October.

Because I greatly respect your opinion, I'd like you to take a few moments to peruse these chapters and e-mail me a short review that I can use for the book.

The book illustrates with elegance and ease how anyone can self-publish a book for less than the cost of going to a vanity press or print-on-demand company.

I've included chapters on choosing a topic, preparing a business plan and outline, writing the manuscript, producing the book, and then selling and marketing the finished product.

Again, I greatly value your opinion, which is why I'd love to have a review from you. If you could have it in my hands by August 12, that would be great. It would allow me time to include it in the layout of the book.

Regards,

I.M. Author

Book Signings

Book signings don't always generate a lot of book sales, but they do give you maximum exposure in a bookstore or another venue.

For a signing in a bookstore, staff might display an author's books in a high-traffic location for the week leading up to the event, and they will certainly post signs with information about the signing and when it will take place.

Often, an author will leave the logistics of attracting people to the book signing in the bookseller's hands. The bookstore might do some local advertising or put up a flyer, but none of this guarantees traffic. It helps if the author takes some initiative and circulates information about the signing to friends and contacts. Don't expect the bookstore to search for organizations, social clubs, and businesses that it can notify with fax or e-mail invitations. This kind of extra effort is up to you.

Even if hordes of readers don't flock to the store to buy your book, you can still use a signing to your advantage. You are creating a relationship with the bookstore manager, for one thing. For another, you never know who is going to walk into that store. It could be someone who hires you to write their next book, a customer interested in a bulk purchase, or your next romantic partner.

Lyle Manery, author of *No Salesman Will Call?*, says:

> Book signings should be fun. I have done several and have always managed to sell books. However, if you sit there like a lump of clay, you will not sell many books. You do have to work at it. The success of the effort cannot be measured by the number of books you actually sell during the time you are present. Sometimes people will come back to buy after you have left. On one occasion, while at the store, I sold 5 books. However, in the week that followed, the store sold 21 books. I have tried advertising before the event, and it brought out some people, but not as many as expected. Of course, if you have friends in the area, it is good to let them know about the event. If you enjoy speaking in front of an audience, giving a free talk pertaining to your book is a great idea, if the store can accommodate it.

Warren Redman agrees:

> I've done lots and planned them to coincide with
> the launch of the book, a presentation/workshop,
> or a conference or other event taking place in the
> locality. I have done signings/talks in bookstores in
> Halifax, Nova Scotia, and Vancouver, among other
> places. Successful? It was a great experience.
> Numbers ranged from 50 to 5. You have exposure
> to the store staff, who are more likely to promote
> the book. The better signings are those at the end
> of presentations and workshops I do.

Canadian Spies author Tom Douglas says,

> I have done several book signings. The first I found
> rather disappointing in that only about 50 people
> turned up (and many were close friends or rela-
> tives), despite the fact many people had voluntarily
> suggested they'd be there and the event was well
> publicized. Another went fairly well. The publisher
> had Gail (my wife) and me sign books at a library
> convention in Toronto, but I was a tad disappoint-
> ed they wouldn't pay mileage for us to travel back
> and forth to Toronto. The lunch break consisted of
> a chit for a less-than-appetizing sandwich and soft
> drink we had to consume sitting on a pile of book
> cartons, because there was no other place to eat the
> stuff. So much for the glamorous life of a writer!
> When Gail was first published with another pub-
> lisher, they flew us to New York. The publisher and
> editor took us to lunch at a trendy Manhattan
> restaurant. We've often thought that if we had been
> born in Sault Ste. Marie, Michigan, instead of
> across the river in the Canadian Soo, we would have
> done much better as authors.

Stan Fischler has also had mixed experiences:

> I've done several [signings]. I knew a manager of a
> bookstore in downtown Manhattan. She's a big
> hockey fan, and I've done signings with her before.
> I called her up and she said, "Let's do it." Some of
> the signings were generated by the PR guy hired for

the book. Others were done by people who found out about me and called me. I usually try to help bring a crowd. I try to promote it as much as possible. I know people who might be interested and call them up. Obviously, there are times you're disappointed. I've been more pleased than disappointed overall. For Denis Potvin's book, I did a book signing across the street from Madison Square Garden. It was very poorly publicized in every way. It was a huge disappointment. He was very upset about it. You can't win them all.

Bruce Dowbiggin claims, "Signings are invariably disastrous to me. [The] best signings were ones that accompanied a talk. Get people to pay, and they'll show up and buy a book." (See the "Speaking Engagements and Workshops" section below.)

Even if your book is not in a bookstore, you can still promote it through book signings in many other locations, including the following:

- Libraries
- Coffee houses
- Retail shops
- Malls
- Flea markets
- Hockey arenas
- Ball diamonds
- Community halls

If you are setting up a signing on your own, you'll want to send press releases (see "Notifying the Media" later in this chapter) to media outlets that might publicize the event. Are there community calendars in your local newspapers or on television or radio stations? Find out what information they need and when they need it to include it in their listings.

Design an eye-catching poster with all relevant information (What's happening? Who's involved? Where and when is it taking place?) that you can post in and around the venue and in nearby stores, community centers, and other places people will see it. Give copies to friends and family to post in their workplaces or apartment buildings. Send out e-mail notices to people on your contact list who live near where you'll be doing the signing.

Learn the dos and don'ts of successful book signings.

Make sure your book fits the venue. In other words, go where your target audience goes. If you've written an accounting book, you're not likely to have much success with a book signing at a hockey rink or ball diamond unless there's a tournament for accountants taking place.

Whether you do a signing at a bookstore or another location, the following are some dos and don'ts:

- Do be prepared to answer a lot of questions.

- Don't sit there and read a newspaper.

- Do look approachable. Smile.

- Don't rely on the venue to supply a pen for signing. Take one with you.

- Do have props to help pique the interest of passersby.

- Do take extra copies of your book that you can sell to the bookstore in case it runs out.

Edie Postill Cole, the author of *Eggs for Shoes,* is a homemaker and grandmother with absolutely no fear of approaching anyone to tell them about her book. She asks everyone within earshot, "Would you like to see the book I wrote?" Then, as they draw nearer to the table, she proceeds to tell them what it is about. Her book is in only a handful of local bookstores and she's had few media interviews, but she travels around to rural communities and does book signings wherever she can. This self-publisher has sold over 5,000 copies.

Speaking Engagements and Workshops

Look for opportunities to speak about your book's topic. The community and business sections of the newspaper often list upcoming events or monthly meetings held by associations and business groups. These organizations, including Lions clubs, Rotary clubs, Kinsmen and Kinette clubs, are always looking for guest speakers. Some business groups have lunch-and-learn series and are constantly in need of innovative speakers. You probably won't be paid for these types of talks (though you may get a free breakfast, lunch, or small gift), but you *will* be developing good contacts, and people in the audience may pass on information about your book to friends and colleagues. There is often also a chance to sell copies of your book at these events.

You can promote your book at seminars and workshops, particularly if it's a self-help, motivational, or business book. One author of local history books has established a viable career for herself by giving workshops for people who want to write family histories. Be creative. These events could be stand-alone sessions that you set up yourself, or you can promote yourself as a speaker for seminars held in conjunction with trade shows, annual general meetings, or other gatherings of industry groups and professional associations.

If you're organizing the event yourself, you'll need to promote it. Refer to the ideas in the previous section on "Book Signings." If you've been asked to speak at a meeting or trade show, it may be closed to the public. If not, the group holding the event will do some promotion, but you may want to let your contact list know about it.

Make sure you plan your speech or workshop thoroughly. Think about the reasons you are doing it for that particular group. You may start with your standard presentation, but fine-tune it to fit the intended audience. For example, if you wrote a children's book and have been asked to speak to a technological firm, you might decide to talk about the technological challenges of publishing.

Don't advertise the event as a seminar and then try to speak off the cuff unless you have done it several times over and are a professional speaker who knows the material inside and out. Even professional speakers plan and go over their material before they speak.

Don't get up and start your talk by saying, "I'm not a very good speaker." If you're not a good speaker, why are you up there? Why shouldn't people bolt from the room right then? If you are not a good speaker, there are numerous sources (ranging from books to groups like Toastmasters) from which you can gather tips to improve your delivery before you step up on that stage. The more confident you are at the podium, the clearer your message will be and the more significant the impression you will leave on the audience. In your own experience, how memorable were the bad speakers you have heard over the years? Do you even remember what they talked about? No? That's my point.

When you speak, don't ramble on about "my book this" and "my book that." Give the audience members some real information they can take home with them — nuggets of inspiration, tips on how to improve their business or home life, suggestions of what to look out for, based on your own experience. It all comes back to having a purpose and a plan before you speak.

When you are going to be speaking to a large group or are organizing your own seminar, find someone who can look after the book sales table. It's difficult to speak and sell books at the same time. Even if you have to pay a neighborhood kid $20 to collect money and issue receipts, it's worth it. If someone else is in charge of sales, you'll be able to concentrate on mingling with the crowd and making a bigger impact after your talk is finished.

Press Conferences

If you have written a book on a topical issue — say, for example, your book contains new information about a political issue that is receiving media attention — you may decide to hold a press conference when the book comes out in order to get that information to the widest audience as soon as possible. Note that the information should be something newsworthy to warrant a press conference.

An organized press conference needs a spokesperson — someone to introduce the speaker and facilitate questions. You should have a podium or a head table if there is more than one speaker. The spokesperson will introduce the speakers and, if they're not all at the front of the room, call them up one at a time. After the speakers have had their say, the spokesperson can take questions from individual reporters before breaking the conference up into one-on-one scrums.

Before a press conference, you should send out a media advisory (see the section on media advisories later in this chapter) to alert the media to its time, place, and subject. You should have a press release, or maybe even a press kit, available on-site for those who attend. A press kit should include a copy of the press release, some background material (biographies, clippings, reviews) on speakers and the issue, perhaps a copy of the media advisory, and sometimes a photograph. Too much information is a waste of trees.

Too much information in a press release is a waste of paper.

You only need enough information to allow a reporter to do the story, with or without interview clips.

When the press conference is over, send copies of the press release or press kit to all the media to catch those who didn't attend.

The following is a list of things you should consider or keep track of when you organize a press event:

- Notify media with a media advisory that you e-mail and/or fax.

- Maintain an RSVP list. (This is especially important if the event includes a lunch, as you'll need to know how much food to order.)

- Keep track of who showed up and who was missing. (Although you will subsequently send out a press release to all outlets, even the ones who attended, you want to make sure you reach the ones that didn't show up.)

- Be aware of what else is going on in your locality — there may be another event going head to head with yours that will be a priority for media.

- Give speakers a time limit for their speech (make sure they stick to it) and find out if they will be available for one-on-one interviews after the press conference.

- Prepare press kits — and media accreditation if the venue and size of the event warrants it (for example, events involving authors like Bill Clinton or Lance Armstrong would merit the distribution of accreditation).

- Make sure there is someone organizing food and drinks.

- Draw up a schedule for the event and keep a list of who's doing what so you don't forget anything.

Note: A lot of organizations complain about having to provide food and refreshments at press conferences and joke that the media won't show up unless there's food. There may be some truth to that, but it is also simply a common courtesy, especially if the press conference is timed to run over the lunch or dinner hour. This may be the only meal reporters eat all day if they are running from event to event. If you were in their place, wouldn't you appreciate it?

Notifying the Media

How do you find a list of media to notify? Search online. If you're looking for technology publications in Arizona or Canada, that's what you'll put in your search engine ("technology publications Arizona"). This is the best way, short of phoning every media outlet, to get up-to-date contact information. When you think of how often people move or are promoted, demoted, fired, or transferred, it's easy to see how outdated print directories can be before they are even published. It may be tedious work, searching for each media organization's website, but it's the only way to ensure your information is correct. However, for some monthly or semi-annual periodicals, the information on their websites may not be current either. You can search online or just pick up the phone and call each outlet to find the right contact person.

Other options may be more time-efficient but may also cost a few pennies. In Canada, Canadian Press has a service called PR Direct, <www.prdirect.ca>, which allows you to send a media advisory or press release to every reporter's desk in every media outlet throughout Canada in French, English, or both languages. PrimeZone, at <www.primezone.com>, is a similar site in the United States.

The Press Release

Sending out a press release is one way to get media attention. The purpose of a press release (also called a news release) is to entice a reporter to write or air a story about you or your message. In large cities, each reporter receives at least 100 to 150 press releases per day. Because of the volume of mail, very little time is spent reading each press release.

It's a good idea to find out which reporters specialize in what areas. For example, if your book is on software development issues, the sports editor and even the news editor may not care about the topic. If you can relate the software development issues to everyday business, send your release to the business editor. Some publications have a technology section that you would also target. Send your release to technology-specific publications. Find out the name of the editor and address your release to that person.

If you send e-mail to the media, don't send attachments. They will likely be deleted by the organization's mail servers to protect

A press release is *not* advertising.

against viruses and spam. Paste your press release in the body of the e-mail.

After you have sent the release, wait a few days and then follow up. Speak to the person to whom you sent the information and ask if he or she received it. If they did not receive the release, offer to send it again. If they did receive it, ask if they are interested in doing a story or book review. Following up is one thing, but hounding is another. Don't stalk or harass the editor.

If the title of your release does not grab the reporter's attention, poof! He or she will hit the delete button or toss it in the recycle bin. If reporters can get past the title, the first paragraph may be the only thing they ever read, even if they decide to do the story.

For this reason, a press release is penned in an inverted pyramid style — main information in the first paragraph or two, with less important information at the bottom. After the title, the first paragraph is the most important part of the press release. You should be able to describe your message clearly and precisely in two to three sentences, so readers can catch your main point without reading any further. The writing and messages have to grab reporters' attention so they will see the benefit to their audience.

A press release is *not* advertising. Anything that sounds or smells like advertising will hit the garbage can faster than you can say "trash." The topic must appeal to that media outlet's audience. It has to be interesting, entertaining, important information, and/or something other reporters would deem important. A new book, product, or company is not necessarily news.

Depending on the content of the press release and the source, room for creativity can be limited. Press releases announcing second-quarter numbers for a public company will be a tad dryer than those announcing new books. However, the relative importance of the company and the significance of the numbers could make a difference in how likely the dry press release will be read and followed up.

The bottom line? The release must sell your idea to the media and get them to follow up the story.

When you write a press release, keep the following tips in mind:

- Have an attention-grabbing headline and lead that summarizes the story.

- Simplify the language so anyone can understand it. If your 12-year-old can't understand your press release, rewrite it until he or she can.

- It's a good idea to use stories instead of statistics or lifeless statements. A story can illustrate the point of your press release.

- Most press releases are bland and dry, and unless they contain information on a high-profile organization or individual, most hit the wastebasket.

- Press releases should be able to stand alone and give the reporter enough information to do the story. (Sometimes a news outlet will print the press release verbatim, as filler, rather than writing its own article. Bear that in mind as you write.)

Format your release following these instructions:

- Press releases should never be more than a page and a half long.

- For press releases that continue to a second page, write "continued on page 2" at the bottom of the first page.

- On the second page, write a one-word "slug" and "page 2" at the top in case the two pages get separated (for example, if your release is about Calgary Flames player Jarome Iginla, write "Iginla/page 2")

- Use ### or -30- to signal the end of the document.

- Use letterhead, date the press release, and for goodness sake, don't forget to include your contact information.

See Sample 9 for an example of a press release.

The Media Advisory

If you are having an event (e.g., a book signing, workshop, seminar, or press conference) that the media might be interested in covering, prepare a media advisory. This is basically an invitation to the media. It should be one page long and should list when and where the event will take place, what it is for, and who will be there (particularly, who will be there whom the media will want to interview). You'll need to specify if there are photo opportunities and if there are special arrangements or details that the media need to know

SAMPLE 9
SAMPLE PRESS RELEASE

PRESS RELEASE

FOR IMMEDIATE RELEASE

FUTURE PROSPECTS: NEW BOOK ON MAJOR JUNIOR HOCKEY
With Foreword by Ron Robison, Western Hockey League commissioner

Take a Tour inside the Lifestyle of Major Junior Hockey
from the Players' Perspective

MY TOWN, Alberta, (October 1, 20--) *Future Prospects* (ISBN 0-9730237-4-0) takes a behind-the-scenes look into the world of major junior hockey and examines some of its unique aspects, such as leaving home at a young age, juggling hockey and travel with school commitments, draft issues, and the importance coaches have on players' careers and their lives.

Players discuss the difficult adjustments they have to make, including the jump from minor hockey to major junior and what it's like to go back to junior after attending a professional hockey camp. The reader is left with a strong inside knowledge of what it's like to be a player, the challenges faced, the lifelong camaraderie, as well as having a few chuckles over some really good stories.

Featuring: Kelly Hrudey, Mike Modano, Jiri Fischer, Ron Robison, Andrew Ference, Ryan Getzlaf, Mike Egener, Doug MacLean, Jacques Lemaire, Ethan Moreau, Nigel Dawes, Mike Ricci, Richard Zednik, Patrice Brisebois, Alex Tanguay, Luc Robitaille, Mike Rathje, Braydon Coburn, and Jamie McLennan, to name a few.

Debbie Elicksen covers the NHL as a freelance writer. She has authored *Inside the NHL Dream* (Freelance Communications, 2002), *Positive Sports* (Freelance Communications, 2003), and *Self-Publishing 101* (Self-Counsel Press, 2005).

-30-

For more information contact:
Debbie Elicksen
Freelance Communications
(555) 249-1240
(555) 249-1241 Fax
debe@freelance.ca
www.freelancepublishing.net

about. For example, will there be room for television cameras? Will parking be available? Will there be one-on-one opportunities? Is it a lunch? Will refreshments be available?

Public Service Announcements

Radio, television, and print media are required to set aside some space and airtime for community messages. These are the types of messages you'll find in a public service announcement (PSA). They are basically used to educate the public, promote nonprofit organizations, and announce a community/nonprofit event. For example, the "stop smoking" ads you see on television are usually PSAs.

As an author, it's unlikely you would be making a public service announcement — perhaps you might if Wal-Mart purchased 10,000 copies of your book (we can dream) to donate to a charity for use as a fundraiser — but it's important you understand the difference between a press release, PSA, and media advisory. Table 2 shows the differences.

TABLE 2
DIFFERENCES BETWEEN A PRESS RELEASE, A MEDIA ADVISORY, AND A PSA

Press Release	PSA	Media Advisory
"Sell" the media on the idea of writing an article	Educate the public	Invite the media to attend an event or press conference
Can't appear as advertising	May advertise nonprofit or community events	Announce a potentially newsworthy event
Looking for media coverage	Looking for free space (advertising) rather than an article	Looking for media attendance at an event
Stands alone — provides enough information to write a short article and is written in inverted pyramid structure	Brief and to the point	Tells who, what, where, when about an upcoming event
Maximum 1½ pages	Maximum 1 page	Maximum 1 page

Media Coverage

First, a word of advice. If you want to get media coverage, whether it's a review of your book or an invitation for you to appear on *Oprah,* you will have to give out free books for promotional purposes. Make sure they go to people who are influential, who can give you something in return (a media interview or review), and who will tell people about you and your book. You're going to come across a few "reviewers" who ask for a copy only to get a free book, so don't hand them out indiscriminately. On the other hand, you don't want to be stingy and refuse to give a free copy to someone who can increase your sales or help you get free promotion. Do your research. If necessary, take someone's name and address and mail a review copy after you've checked out their credentials. But be advised, there are more media companies than we can count and many freelance writers work for bona fide outlets. If you are hesitant to send a book, it could turn them off and quash your hopes of publicity from that quarter. Some media outlets will also ask for more than one copy. Before I managed to book a date for the *Vicki Gabereau Show,* I ended up couriering three copies of my book to the producers. It was worth it because I did get on the show and the interview was great.

Book Reviews

Do readers rely on book reviews? To answer that, you might want to ask your friends and family. It's possible a review doesn't make much difference unless it's written by someone they particularly admire and respect. Using a hockey example, if Wayne Gretzky endorsed a product, people might run out and buy it. But if defenseman Jason Marshall endorsed it, the fact that he plays in the National Hockey League might help, but he may not be well known enough to make much of an impact.

On the other hand, a book review is often the only warning some people have that a book exists which may be of interest to them. In such cases, even a bad review can generate sales, as people may buy the book simply because of its subject. If it's fiction, everyone has their own opinion about what they like, so something the reviewer mentions may capture their interest.

It's usually a good idea to send out a limited number of books as review copies to media you have specifically targeted . You want to focus on newspapers, magazines, newsletters, and other media outlets that will reach your book's intended audience.

Make sure these outlets actually *do* book reviews. If they don't, you may have more luck pitching your book as the subject of a news story or an article (see the next section).

Soliciting book reviews from a newspaper or well-known publishing source means competition with other books. How will your proposal stand out amongst the 100 to 150 daily requests? Go back to your press release and make it as to-the-point and compelling as possible. Even so, there is no guarantee you'll get a call or a review.

The best way to get the media's attention is to find an intriguing angle.

Getting Interviewed

While all forms of media do feature new book releases from time to time, before you run out and call every radio and television station to get them to do a segment on your book, it's important to *understand* the media and the service they provide. Use the same technique you use for seeking a publisher or distributor: know their specialty. Go to websites to check out the formats and to see what types of stories each media outlet has featured in the past. If there are archived interviews, review them.

What is news? News is important to the reader, listener, or viewer. It's not about you. News is interesting and entertaining. News is something other reporters deem important.

What is not news? New products, new services, and advertising are not news. Business owners think that just because they started a new business, it's news. Unless a product or service will revolutionize people's lives, it's not likely going to be seen as news — except in trade media that focus on the specific industry the product or service is aimed at.

What news captures your attention? Next time you are reading a paper, watching television, listening to the radio, or browsing a news outlet's website, pay attention to which stories draw you in. Why did you notice them? Use that knowledge when you prepare your own media plan.

The best way to get the media's attention is to find an intriguing angle. Human interest, advice, a gimmick, good stories — these are what people want to see, hear, and read.

You can piggyback your book onto another story. For example, Bruce Dowbiggin's book *Money Players: How Hockey's Greatest Stars Beat the NHL at Its Own Game* was released in late 2003, just a year before the National Hockey League lockout obliterated the 2004–05 season. *Money Players* garnered attention as the lockout loomed and hockey fans tried to make sense of the impasse in collective bargaining between the NHL owners and the NHL Players Association. If the lockout had been averted, media interested in the book would have dropped precipitously, but because the lockout did happen, the book enjoyed a longer shelf life, and Dowbiggin was able to maximize his publicity efforts.

If your book is a sales or marketing book, your angle may be "helping others reach their potential." If your company is an accounting firm, you can offer tips on "how to beat the taxman." These are angles the general public will find interesting. You can sell these angles to the media with a compelling argument that convinces them you will be an interesting interviewee who will make huge numbers of people tune in to their show or read their publication.

Here are some other angles to get the media interested in your book:

- Respond to an event that's making headlines (e.g., Kitty Kelley's timely books on political controversy).

- Use statistics to tie into a survey (the facts in your book can enhance media coverage of the issue).

- Present a local angle ("Local author discovers the secret to long-term relationships").

- Comment on an industry trend (set yourself up as the industry expert).

- Perform a public service (offer tips, take a leadership role in your industry).

- Target media specific to the industry or trade you are writing about.

Making a Pitch

Sending out a press release about your book is one way to get the media's attention. Another method is to pitch the topic of your book, rather than the book itself. A pitch is basically a proposal. It is a letter you send to the reporter, introducing yourself and the topic. This can be effective publicity when you have no immediate deadline or need. In other words, your pitch is something the reporter could pick up any time. There is no urgency or "best before" date.

Jill Lublin, a self-described publicity expert, has lots of advice about approaching the media:

> I think the biggest misconception about media is that they want to write about your book, that they care about what you're pitching. They have an audience to reach. They need to deliver value to their readers, viewers, and listeners. I think people just assume that the media are just going to open the door and say yes.
>
> The other misconception is that when they say no, you ought to just stop — that no means no. Well, no means no for just that minute. Go back in and repitch the media. The other thing people feel about the media is, "Well, I'm bugging them." It's your job to bug them. In *Guerrilla Publicity*, we talk about the rule of seven, which is to pitch the media at least seven times. Do not stop until you've done that at least seven times with a pitch.
>
> It's important you get started on publicity for your book way before you need it. Do not wait for your book to come out. With *Guerrilla Publicity*, we started on PR nine months ahead. On *Networking Magic* we did the same. I think if you want really great results, you have to start way ahead.
>
> Be willing to do whatever it takes for publicity. Wake up at 5:30 in the morning — I've done several radio interviews like that. Stay an extra day in a city. Make sure you develop some speaking platforms and some ongoing visibility. You need to keep an eye on what it is you're going to create in your campaign for quite a bit of time. Don't just go, "Oh, my book came out, so that's it." Keep your foot on the gas consistently. Be willing to really put it out there so that you can let people know who you are.

When media seek interviews for television and radio, they are looking for people with a strong message who can be entertaining.

If you don't like the news, go out and make some of your own. Make it up with your book, with who you are, your expertise. Remember, you are an expert. The question is, what are you an expert in?

The advice I've given to people with media interviews is, get clear about what problems you solve. It's not about the book you're writing. It's really about the problem you solve and the solution you would recommend to people. If they're reading the newspaper, listening to the radio, or watching TV, they want to know what they can do. As one ABC producer told me when I interviewed her for *Guerrilla Publicity*, "Jill, just tell us what we can do. I want to keep my viewers from changing the channel." It's really important to be clear that the media are not all about promoting your book. They're about giving their readers, viewers, and listeners answers to problems.

As Jill says, a television or radio show or a newspaper feature writer isn't interested in *you*. When media seek interviews for television and radio, they are looking for people with a strong message who can be entertaining. They want a hot topic, something current and newsworthy. They want you to solve a problem, talk about a controversial issue, dispel a myth, or introduce an innovative idea. Whatever the topic is, it has to be relevant to the audience you are pitching to. You may end up tweaking your topic to fit several different media outlets.

It's not just about pitching a topic, either. You need to have some expertise behind you in order to talk about it. Perhaps that expertise is your book, but in most cases it's connected to your life. Always include anything that boosts your credibility when making a media pitch.

Always know more about the media outlet than its employees know about you, especially if you are going for a national outlet. The more you can customize your pitch, the better your shot at getting in. Make sure you watch or listen to a few episodes to get a better understanding of what they are looking for in a guest. If you're looking for a print interview, know what the reporter you're pitching to has published.

Answer the following questions in order to tailor your pitch to the outlet:

- What is the format of the show?

- Who are the hosts and what is their background?

- What types of stories do they feature?

- Who have some of their guests been?

- Where do you fit in?

- If your topic has been covered before, can you approach it from a different angle?

If you don't know who to contact for the show, watch the credits. The information may or may not be available online. If you're still unsure, you could even call or e-mail the show for that information.

Producers and editors don't have time to sift through pages of material. Keep your pitch to one page — two at the most. You're selling the idea, not your book's contents or your life story. What makes your idea stand out from the others? Why should they choose you? Remember, it's not about you, it's about the audience.

If you're pitching to a national television audience, or if the popularity of a local show merits it, you might want to prepare a demo video containing interview clips that show what a good interview you can give and how interesting you will be for their audience.

Prepare talking points you want to get across — probably six at the most. This isn't something you necessarily share with the media. Keep it handy when you are being interviewed. It keeps you on track with your message.

Understand the power and limitations of freelance reviewers. Never assume, just because someone freelances, that he or she is not worth the same amount of your attention as an employee of a mainstream media organization, and that they shouldn't receive the same information. Most of the well-known media outlets use freelancers for gathering stories. Of course, there are also those who call themselves reviewers after posting a few reviews on a hastily thrown-together website, so they can solicit accreditation to sought-after events, but a little digging will help you figure out which is which.

When the Media Call

When the media do call, the worst thing you can do is make it difficult for them to connect with you. Be available. If you're not, they'll wonder why you contacted them in the first place.

Be prepared. There is nothing worse for a reporter or interviewer than unprepared subjects who can't answer the simplest of questions — particularly if it's about their own book.

When you do land a media interview, make the best of it. Be interesting and speak in short sentences. Prepare, prepare, prepare. Yes, you wrote the book, but unless you have a photographic memory, you're not going to remember every word you wrote.

Contrary to popular belief, you don't have your book pages memorized. That was always one of my biggest fears when doing a live television or radio interview . What if they asked me a question I couldn't answer? What a doofus I'd look like if I didn't know what was in my own book.

Go to the interview with simple handheld notes that remind you of a story that will interest the reader, listener, or viewer. But keep it simple. Don't go into such detail that the interviewer has to give you the hook.

If you disagree with something the interviewer says, don't be confrontational. Use diplomacy and come up with a story or other example to make your point. Don't let interviewers lose face by belittling them or telling them they are wrong.

It's a good idea to pitch to local media before branching out nationally. That way, you can improve your on-air skills and get comfortable with being interviewed. The biggest lesson you'll learn is you don't have as much time as you thought you would to convey your message. Doing a few local interviews first will help you hone your message so you can get it across completely and concisely by the time you're getting national coverage.

As with any public speaking, preparation builds confidence. Practice talking in short and articulate sentences. If you're on television, maintain eye contact with the host. Be yourself. Pretend it's just you and the interviewer having a coffee at the mall.

If you are doing a print interview, there's a little less pressure. You're not in front of a camera, so you don't have to worry about getting your point across as quickly (though you still don't want to ramble), and if you forget something or don't know the answer to a question, you can always go home, look up the information, and phone it in to the reporter. In a situation like that, get back to them with the answer within the hour, and make sure you get it to the right person. Media work on deadlines. If you drag your feet getting back to them with the information they need to complete the story, your story could be killed.

Media can help you a lot if you use them correctly. Always be respectful and well prepared. If you are a good interviewee, you have a better chance of getting media coverage for your next project. And never underestimate the power of what you may perceive as smaller, insignificant outlets. Local cable television can be one of your best sources for publicity. I can't tell you how many people say to me that they saw me on the local community cable channel after an interview. I've been on the community cable station numerous times. Sometimes people may not remember what the book was about or why you were on, but they remember you. That in itself is a great feeling.

10
Conclusion

Book publishing can be daunting, expensive, and frustrating. It can also be wonderful and intoxicating when you see your finished book on your bookshelf. It's especially satisfying if you know your book has made a difference in someone's life — even just one reader — but the hours, costs, and low return can give you second thoughts. Many of the authors and self-publishers I talked to expressed this ambivalence.

Stan Fischler:

> For the most part, the lesson is the amount of work that is put in does not have an equivalent amount of satisfaction monetarily. Mostly, it's a labor of love.

Warren Redman:

> I waited too long before looking at the marketing side. This needs to be considered right at the out-set. Also, printing too many [copies]of the first book I self-published. Writing a book and selling it are totally different concepts. You use a different part of your brain.

Bruce Dowbiggin:

> Don't write or research too much. Have a very clear idea what you're doing and be ruthless in editing. Less is virtually always more. And it's cheaper ...

Keep writing and don't stop. When you find a patron, ride them.

Ron and Adrianna Edwards:

When considering topics for a book, consider making the scope as broad as possible. Will this subject be of interest outside your town? Is it nationwide? What about international appeal?

You may well be the next Stephen King, but chances are you're not. It is extremely difficult to make a living by writing or publishing books in Canada. Most of us do it for the love, not the money, but you still have to treat it as a business. If you are not making money writing/producing books, then it is a hobby, which is fine for many.

Tom Douglas:

My expensive lesson was the cost of mailing [books] to buyers and the realization that a lot of people you know expect a freebie. I have had to tell a couple of my mooching friends that for my self-published book, I had to pay the entire bill, and with the others, I only get ten free copies and those I use for promotional purposes. Anything above that, I have to pay for. When they give me a hard time about it, I ask them if they would walk into a friend's clothing store and expect to get a free suit, or into a friend's restaurant and expect him to pick up the tab for the meal.

Unless you're a masochist who enjoys having people who have trouble spelling "accommodate" sitting in judgment on something you sweated over for months or years, don't get into writing. And don't think you're going to get rich at it unless you're one in a million who has an absolutely unique idea — or you happen to hit the right trend at the right time.

Jill Lublin:

The expensive lesson I learned was, if you are writing a book with a partner, be clear about who does what and what you're going to spend. We didn't have a budget pre-prepared for *Guerrilla Publicity.* I spent a great deal of money publicizing it, buying media lists, buying lists to send postcards to. Those are things I didn't necessarily do for the second book, *Networking Magic.* We still got a great deal of publicity in places like *The New York Times,* and *Entrepreneur Magazine.* We got great publicity on *Guerrilla Publicity.* But I'll tell you, because I didn't preplan a budget and really didn't think it all the way through, I did find myself spending more money on the first book than I probably should have spent. I did not do that for the second book. I also did a huge e-mail campaign, which helped *Guerrilla Publicity,* which went number seven on Amazon. When you're on the top ten books, you immediately become a bestseller. Because we learned how to do the e-mail campaign more effectively, *Networking Magic* actually went number one on Barnes & Noble three weeks in a row. That was very exciting.

The difference between success and failure often depends on how much effort you're willing to invest.

As you can see, publishing a book has little to do with what's between the covers. It's all about sales. Whether you go through a traditional publisher or publish it yourself, the process is the same. You need an outline. You need a plan — a marketing plan. You need to take the initiative and create your own publicity.

It's not an easy task, and it can be an expensive venture. If you really believe in your message, do a bang-up job of making the physical product attractive, and look for additional ways to promote your book apart from bookstores, you'll be successful.

The difference between success and failure often depends on how much effort you're willing to invest.

When you're in a rut, here are some points to keep you grounded:

- Believe in yourself — write down your affirmations every night before you go to bed and when you wake — say them to yourself continuously.

- Reevaluate. Are you targeting the right market? Do your goals still apply? Do you need to revisit how you're approaching people? Get tips and ideas from sales and marketing books.

- Motivate yourself with motivating material. Collect uplifting quotes and stick them to your computer or mirror.

- Pat yourself on the back for the things you have done well and the fact you have accomplished something so many others just talk about doing.

- Diversify — don't get stuck in one direction.

- Take some time for yourself and relax; have fun, watch a football game or a movie, pet the cat.

If you're ready to give up, think about the story of Saku Koivu. In September 2001, the Montreal Canadiens' center announced he had cancer — non-Hodgkin's lymphoma. Pittsburgh Penguins star Mario Lemieux, who had been diagnosed with Hodgkin's disease several years earlier, held a press conference along with one of Koivu's closest friends, Mark Recchi. They wanted to support the Montreal player as he prepared for the challenging days ahead. In the course of the event, Lemieux said that a positive attitude had had everything to do with his own recovery. He believed that the mind could cure disease.

After a long and extensive treatment, Koivu beat the odds and returned to the Habs lineup for their last three games. He played a leading role in all 12 playoff games.

Koivu could have given up. His determination to get back into the NHL is what drove him to recovery. He is living proof that perseverance can beat any odds to achieve success.

What's stopping you from following *your* desires? Do you really want to write that book? If so, why are you listening to those negative voices? Think positive, do your research, and write that book!

Appendix 1
Self-Publishing Resources

These are just a handful of resources you can access for more information about publishing, writing, editing, and project management. To find more sources, go to an Internet search engine such as Google, at <www.google.com>, and key in what you're looking for.

Books and Articles

Bernays, Anne, and Pamela Painter. *What If? Writing Exercises for Fiction Writers.* New York: HarperCollins, 1990.

Clements, Wayne. *The Selling Edge: A Consultative Approach.* Calgary: BTW Management Corporation, 2004.

Hopkins, Tom. *How to Master the Art of Selling.* New York: Warner Books Edition, 1982.

Publishers Marketing Association and Book Industry Study Group. *The Rest of Us 2003: An Update of the 1998 Report on America's Independent, Smaller Book Publishers.* Available from Publishers Marketing Association <www.pma-online.org/benefits/whitepapers.cfm>.

Sharp, Caroline. *A Writer's Workbook: Daily Exercises for the Writing Life.* New York: St. Martin's Press, 2000.

Suzanne, Claudia. "The Good Life of Ghostwriting." *WritersWeekly,* October 3, 2001, <www.writers weekly.com/this _weeks_article/000607_10032001.html>.

Whiting, Percy H. *The 5 Great Rules of Selling.* New York: Dale Carnegie & Associates, 1974.

Web Resources

Bookstores

Booksellers' Associations

American Booksellers Association: www.bookweb.org

Canadian Booksellers Association: www.cbabook.org/find/default.asp

Online Bookstores

Amazon: www.amazon.com

Barnes & Noble: www.barnesandnoble.com

Booklocker: www.booklocker.com

Chapters/Indigo: www.chapters.indigo.ca

eBookstand: www.ebookstand.com

CIP Programs and ISBNs

Canadian ISBN Agency: www.collectionscanada.ca/isbn/

Library and Archives Canada Cataloguing in Publication Program: www.collectionscanada.ca/cip/

Library of Congress Cataloging in Publication Progam: cip.loc.gov

US ISBN Agency: www.isbn.org

Copyright Information

Access Copyright: www.accesscopyright.ca

Canadian Intellectual Property Office: www.cipo.gc.ca

Copyright Clearance Center: www.copyright.com

US Copyright Office: www.copyright.gov

Editing

Chicago Manual of Style: www.press.uchicago.edu/Misc/Chicago/cmosfaq/cmosfaq.html

Editors' Association of Canada: www.editors.ca

University of Wisconsin-Madison Writing Center: www.wisc.edu/writing/Handbook/index.html

Indexing

American Society of Indexers: www.asindexing.org

Indexing and Abstracting Society of Canada: www.indexingsociety.ca

Industry News and Sources

Adler & Robin Books: www.adlerrobin.com, www.adlerbooks.com

Association of Authors' Representatives: www.aar-online.org

Book Industry Study Group: www.bisg.org

Bookwire: www.bookwire.com

Para Publishing: www.parapub.com

Publishers Lunch: www.publisherslunch.com

Publishers Weekly: www.publishersweekly.com

Publishing Central: www.publishingcentral.com

Research and Markets: www.researchandmarkets.com

Statistics Canada: www.statcan.ca

Libraries

Canadian Library Gateway: www.collectionscanada.ca/gateway

Library and Archives Canada: www.collectionscanada.ca

Library of Congress: www.loc.gov

Libweb: lists.webjunction.org/libweb/

PublicLibraries.com: www.publiclibraries.com

Marketing and Promotion

American Marketing Association: www.marketingpower.com

Book Marketing Works: www.bookmarketingworks.com

Clements Consulting Group: www.clementsgroup.com

Guerrilla Marketing Coach: www.gmarketingcoach.com

Tom Hopkins International: www.tomhopkins.com

KnowThis.com: www.knowthis.com

Jill Lublin: www.promisingpromotion.com

MarketingProfs: www.marketingprofs.com

Ed Osworth's Internet Marketing Index: www.internetmarketingindex.com

PubInsider.com: www.pubinsider.com

George Torok (co-author of *Secrets of Power Marketing*): www.torok.com

The Write News: www.writenews.com

Print-on-Demand Publishers, Vanity Presses, E-Publishers

AuthorHouse: www.authorhouse.com

Dorrance Publishing: www.dorrancepublishing.com

iUniverse: www.iuniverse.com

Trafford Publishing: www.trafford.com

Vantage Press: www.vantagepress.com

Xlibris: www2.xlibris.com

Publishing

Association of American Publishers: www.publishers.org

Association of Book Publishers of British Columbia — Self-Publishing Information: www.books.bc.ca/selfpublishing.php

Association of Canadian Publishers: www.publishers.ca

Canadian Publishers' Council: www.pubcouncil.ca

Independent Publishers Association of Canada: www.ipac-publishers.com

PMA, the Independent Book Publishers Association: www.pma-online.org

Small Publishers Association of North America: www.spannet.org

WritersServices — Manuscript to Reader: www.writersservices.com/wps/m_script_to_reader.htm

Writing

Absolute Write: www.absolutewrite.com

Canadian Authors Association: www.canauthors.org

Canadian Centre for Studies in Publishing: www.ccsp.sfu.ca

Journalism.org: www.journalism.org

Science Fiction and Fantasy Writers of America: www.sfwa.org

Wordwrights Canada — Canadian Links of Interest to Writers: www3.sympatico.ca/susanio/WWClinks.html

Writers Online Workshops: www.writersonlineworkshops.com

WritersWeekly: www.writersweekly.com

Writtenword.org: www.writtenword.org

Exporting Books

If you plan to export books from Canada into the United States, check out the cargo security program called C-TPAT (Customs–Trade Partnerships Against Terrorism). Participating in this program might eliminate delays at the border, particularly if your carrier is considered high risk. Go to the website for more information: www.customs.gov/xp/cgov/import/commercial_enforcement/ctpat/.

Customs spot-checks shipments in and out of the country — particularly from Canada to the United States, so it's important to make sure you have the country of origin listed on the carton label and inside each book. You'll show it as "Printed in the USA" or "Printed in Canada."

Clearing books through customs could offer a challenge. It's best to have all the requirements met up front. Contact your distributor to confirm details and use a shipper that can easily handle customs on your behalf.

Appendix 2
Test Your Editing Skills

Answers to these exercises can be found at the end of this appendix.

Punctuation

Which phrase is wrong, or are they both right?

Women's rights	Womens' rights
Cold roast beef	Cold, roast, beef
She was a 12-year-old girl.	She was a 12 year old girl.

Tighten Up
Part 1

Improve on the following sentences. Note: There isn't one correct version, but by looking at the sample answers, you can see how you can make your sentences crisper and easier to read.

1. Not meeting the deadline will put the project in jeopardy.

2. We gave careful consideration to this proposal.

3. He gave no indication which format he had a preference for.

4. I'll make every effort to finish the report by Thursday.

5. The technical vocabulary of the article causes reader confusion.

Part 2

You can see how deleting awkward repetitions and rewriting the following sentences in a parallel form sharpens them. For example:

Instead of: Sally rode the roller coaster. Sally threw up.

Write this: Sally rode the roller coaster and threw up.

1. I found it easier to write the book than editing it.

2. The forms should be read first, accurately completed, and then you should return them to the administrator.

3. Tommy handled the customer complaint quickly, thoroughly, and he was very professional.

Which/Witch Word?

I was writing an article about a housing development and the term "palette" was used with respect to the array of colors available for home exteriors. The client asked me to double-check the spelling. If we weren't confused before, we sure were after I uncovered the following list of definitions from the *Webster's New World Dictionary, Third College Edition:*

- Palate: Roof of mouth, sense of taste

- Palette: Thin board or tablet of wood or plastic, often with a hole at one end for thumb; arranges and mixes paint; the colors used by a particular artist for painting

- Pallet: Wooden tool consisting of flat blade with handle; small bed or pad filled with straw; vertical stripe half as wide as a pale

- Palette: Low, portable platform on which materials are stacked

- Pallette: Plate protecting the armpit

Some words are confusing. When in doubt, look it up.

1. In his presentation, Jack (inferred, implied) that he would volunteer for the job.

2. The increasing (influence, affluence) of the strike has had an unfortunate (affect, effect) on the subcontractors who want the work.

3. His shoes (complement/compliment) his pants and shirt nicely.

4. The (capitol/capital) of Washington is Seattle.

Answers

Punctuation

The phrases on the left are correct.

Tighten Up

Part 1

1. Missing the deadline puts the project in jeopardy.
2. We carefully considered the proposal.
3. He had no format preference.
4. Expect the report by Thursday.
5. The article's technical vocabulary confuses the reader.

Part 2

1. The book was easier to write than edit.
2. Return your forms to the administrator after you've read and accurately completed them.
3. Tommy was very professional in handling the customer complaint quickly and thoroughly.

Which/Witch Word?

1. To imply is to hint that he will do the job, whereas to infer is to draw a conclusion that he will do the job.
2. Influence is the power to affect others. Affluence is abundance. Affect is a verb (to influence), and effect is a noun (result).
3. Complement completes the wardrobe. Compliment is flattery or praise.
4. A capitol is a building. Capital, in this case, is the seat of government.